No Longer Slaves

No Longer Slaves

Galatians and African American Experience

Brad Ronnell Braxton

A Michael Glazier Book

THE LITURGICAL PRESS
Collegeville, Minnesota

www.litpress.org

A Michael Glazier Book published by The Liturgical Press.

Cover design by Keith McCormick.

2	3	4	5	6	7	8

Library of Congress Cataloging-in-Publication Data

Braxton, Brad Ronnell.
    No longer slaves : Galatians and African American experience / Brad Ronnell Braxton.
       p. cm.
    "A Michael Glazier book."
    Includes bibliographical references (p.   ) and index.
    ISBN 0-8146-5948-9
      1. Bible. N.T. Galatians—Reader-response criticism.   2. African Americans—Religion.   I. Title.

BS2685.52 .B73   2002
227'.406'08996073—dc21

                                        2002067633

Contents

Acknowledgments

This work has had two incarnations—one as a university thesis and another as a piece of public scholarship distributed (I hope) to a wide audience. In each instance there have been persons whose insight, expertise, and inspiration contributed immensely to the process. In this volume's "first life" Christopher Rowland and Peter Henry served as invaluable dialogue partners as I hammered out methodological concerns.

Also, I must mention the assistance of Itumeleng Mosala, a noted South African Old Testament scholar. During the spring term in 1992 I visited him while he was on sabbatical leave at Cambridge University. The afternoon spent conversing and dreaming with him about this project looms large in my memory. Additionally, I am grateful to Trevón Gross for his consistent friendship. Trevón's priceless computer knowledge facilitated the production of my Oxford thesis. In addition, David Ball, Isaac Diggs, and Sean Winter provided valuable editorial assistance.

A host of persons also contributed to this volume's "second life." David DeSilva of Ashland Theological Seminary suggested that I send the manuscript to The Liturgical Press. Linda Maloney, Academic Editor at The Liturgical Press, eagerly received my project and with great patience guided it to completion. Moreover, I am grateful to President Thomas K. Hearn, Jr. and Dean Bill Leonard of Wake Forest University for their support and encouragement of my scholarship and teaching. Also, I am deeply appreciative of Sherry Magill and Edward King, Jr., of the Jessie Ball duPont Fund for the generous endowment of my professorial post at Wake Forest University Divinity School.

The students in my "Corinthian Correspondence" course at Wake Forest Divinity School in the spring of 2001 read a version of Chapter

Two. They helped me to think more critically about reading the Bible as "Scripture." Edgar McKnight of Furman University read the entire manuscript. Michael Brown of Emory University and Ayo Adewuya of the Church of God Theological Seminary read portions of it. Their suggestions and corrections were enormously helpful. Heather Cronk and Daniel Miles edited the bibliography. Additionally, Vanessa Willis's editorial prowess significantly enhanced the clarity of this book. I hold all these "collaborators" responsible for any strengths of the book. The reader may hold *me* responsible for any weaknesses in it.

I am indebted immeasurably to my parents, the Rev. James and Mrs. Louise Braxton, for their abundant love and exemplary Christian witness. Perhaps the greatest blessing they have bestowed upon me was introducing me to the African American church, that desert oasis where black pilgrims have found hope and healing.

Finally, if ever I doubted that God is good, that doubt was forever erased July 6, 1996—the day I met my wife, Lazetta. I am sustained by her love, energized by her zest, and constantly challenged by her prophetic discernment. With gratitude I dedicate this book to her. Thank you, Lazetta, for teaching me that simplicity and profundity can be best friends.

Preface

I began the research for this book while completing my master of philosophy degree in New Testament studies at the University of Oxford, England. I owe an enormous intellectual debt to my Oxford supervisor and dear friend, Professor Christopher Rowland. His guidance, encouragement, critical questioning, and sympathetic listening helped me bring this project to fruition. I shall never forget the watershed conversation we had one autumn evening in 1992 when we both were seized by the mysteries of our ethnic and cultural differences. We allowed those differences to fuel this research project and to deepen our friendship.

When I traveled to Oxford in the fall of 1991 to study theology on a Rhodes Scholarship I had no idea that I would be allowed to write such an unconventional thesis. When one thinks of the University of Oxford one usually conjures up images of conservative British dons strolling the cobblestone streets. I did meet my share of traditional Oxford dons, and they added to the spirit and mystique of that ancient university.

As divine providence would have it, however, Christopher Rowland would be assigned as my graduate supervisor. To be sure, he is an internationally renowned New Testament scholar, but, as I would soon find out, he is in no way a conservative Oxford don. As a committed liberation theologian Professor Rowland is as comfortable talking about the contemporary (and even revolutionary) implications of the Christian message as he is discussing the historical and social exigencies that spawned early Christianity. As I sat in his study at the Queen's College week after week in our one-to-one teaching sessions I learned from him an axiom that informs this present work and all my thinking about New Testament studies.

Professor Rowland taught me that biblical interpretation is an act of politics. I intend no irreverence by this statement. It only underscores the enduring religious and cultural influence the Bible exerts upon countless societies in the world. Even in a postmodern age that is skeptical of Truth with a capital "T," individuals and groups realize that having the Bible on their side can be a very persuasive rhetorical move. Thus those who would interpret the Bible, be they Sunday school teachers or university exegetes, are enlisted in the power struggle of declaring what God has said and is saying in these religious texts. Regardless of one's beliefs about the Bible, millions still look to it to illumine and even organize their realities. Thus any time we dare to say: "This biblical passage means . . .", the balance of power in various communities may be altered.

Given Professor Rowland's interest in contemporary appropriations of the New Testament, he was a well-suited dialogue partner for my quest to offer a reading of the New Testament that takes seriously the past and present experiences of African Americans. As I was generating research ideas I had the good fortune to take my first trip to Mother Africa. In April 1992 I traveled to the Gambia with my trusted friend and Oxford colleague, Peter Henry. One morning during that trip, as I sat on the porch of our hostel room in Banjul, I was reading the Greek text of Galatians. I had read Galatians many times in the past, but this time Paul's words in Gal 4:7, "You are no longer a slave," took on new significance.

As I meditated on those words in the warm air of the Gambia—the homeland of some of my African ancestors and the land from which the slave traders stole thousands of Africans to sell in the Americas and the Caribbean—an epiphany washed over me. Although chattel slavery in America had ended well over a hundred years ago, another form of slavery, ideological in nature but still vicious, continued to hold countless African Americans in a vise-grip. So many African Americans were (and are) shackled by conscious and subconscious capitulations to white ways of thinking and being.

I thought, "An 'ideological Emancipation Proclamation' might be needed." Just as Paul told the Galatians that they were no longer slaves, perhaps, someone needed to remind African Americans of the same truth. The issues with which Paul struggled in the first century and with which African Americans were struggling in the late twentieth century were not identical, but I felt that there was enough similarity between the two to effect a creative conversation. Thus I set out to read this

ancient letter in ways that might shine a beacon of liberation upon contemporary African American experience.

My tenure as a graduate student at the University of Oxford certainly exacerbated my existential need to interpret the New Testament
in the context of my African American experience. As grateful as I was
for the coveted privilege to study at Oxford, I was constantly aware
while there that I was living and studying in one of the ideological
centers of white, dominant culture. During those years I was not the
victim of overt prejudice, but in subtle and sometimes not so subtle
ways the message was conveyed that white cultural experiences were *the*
measuring rod. Being surrounded so intensely by "whiteness," I felt
compelled to realize and articulate my "blackness."

Having grown up in a predominantly white suburban community
in Virginia and having matriculated at the University of Virginia as an
undergraduate, I was no stranger to being the "minority." Yet even in
those settings I found refuge in the validating love of my family and my
church. Frankly, the black church has defined much of my life's purpose.

Rarely did a Sunday pass in my youth that I did not find myself sitting
in the pew of a black Baptist church. This is partly explained because
my father was the pastor of the Baptist church where I grew up and my
mother was a gifted and strong lay leader in that church. Unlike some
youth who found church attendance onerous, I considered it an exciting
opportunity.

The fervent worship, the fiery religious rhetoric, and the spiritual
nurture offered to me by the seasoned "mothers and fathers" of the
church, some of whom had limited formal education but who possessed Ph.D.s in "mother wit," enriched me in ways I cannot articulate.
When I was nineteen, after my first year at the University of Virginia, my
home church granted me my Baptist minister's license, which autho-
rized me to preach whenever asked. Thus it was not unusual during my
undergraduate days for me to preach on Sundays. The care of my family
and the charisma of my religious experience gave me more than enough
courage to fend off any encroachments of prejudice from the dominant
culture.

Later, during my two-year sojourn at the University of Oxford,
I raised the query asked by Israelite exiles over two millennia ago: "How
can we sing the Lord's song in a strange land?" Obviously my family still
loved and supported me, and saints from the church prayed for me and
sent care packages to England, but I felt geographically and existentially

"cut off" from the supply of my strength, most notably the sustaining energy of African American worship.

After much searching, some of my Oxford colleagues and I located a Jamaican nondenominational church where we worshiped regularly. The pastor and people of this church warmly welcomed us into their community, and the worship experiences served as a stabilizing surrogate during my season of exile. Yet some of the isolation I felt did not abate, partly because I rarely had an opportunity to preach while at Oxford, since I lacked the professional connections that I enjoyed in the United States.

At heart I am as much a black preacher who does theology and biblical scholarship as I am a theologian and biblical scholar who preaches. It is nearly impossible to explain, but the cycle of preparing and delivering sermons in the African American congregational setting is as exhilarating as it is demanding. Even when I was physically apart from the African American church during my Oxford years, my unwavering commitment to and longing for the African American spiritual tradition gave overwhelming shape and substance to this project.

Anyone familiar with the African American church and its celebrated preaching tradition knows that African American Christians expect and demand of their preachers spiritual truth that is biblically-focused, socially relevant, rhetorically polished, and emotionally riveting. These expectations are so much a part of my psyche that they apply for me whether I am seeking for truth in homiletical or exegetical work. In short, my tradition has taught me that the spiritual truth that emanates from faithful biblical interpretation must meet the same standards as that which emanates from faithful preaching.

As will be clearly seen in the following interpretations, the boundaries for me between exegesis and proclamation are certainly blurred, and at times nonexistent. When I was completing the initial research for this manuscript at Oxford, Professor Rowland said to me, "In this thesis I hear the voice of a black preacher. This is a voice that the academy needs to hear." In my initial research and even in the process of revision for publication, I have sought to insure that the voice of this black preacher reverberates clearly. This book was written *in* the academy, *and* it was also written *for* the black church.

I recently published my first book, *The Tyranny of Resolution: I Corinthians 7:17-24*, which presents the research from my Emory University doctor of philosophy dissertation in its most technical form. After hearing me go on for months and years about this detailed research in the

Corinthian correspondence my wife Lazetta, who is my most trusted confidante, politely said, "In your next book, make sure that you write something that the rest of us can read." In this present volume I am trying to honor my wife's request. Of course, when Lazetta offered this observation she in no way was asking for a text that skates around and over intellectual complexities. Instead, she was reminding me that there are many ways to demonstrate intellectual rigor and fulfill my vocation as a scholar for the church. There is a hunger, she contends, for theological scholarship that is simple without being simplistic, and challenging without being inaccessible.

In this book I have tried to navigate two very present dangers of intellectual writing—too much documentation and too little documentation. The more expertise one gathers in an intellectual discipline, the more difficult it becomes to say anything without making copious qualifications. A plethora of footnotes, contrary to popular opinion, is not always scholarly flamboyance.

Often thorough scholarly documentation is a tangible sign of humility, the halting realization that others have thought previously about these issues and often have done so more clearly and profoundly than I ever could. Yet in composing this book I realized that if I became overly engrossed in documentation the unusual perspective I was bringing to this material could easily get drowned out by the history of other voices. Unless I showed some restraint, this book could unwittingly have become a history of interpretation instead of *my* interpretation.

Moreover, it may also be a serious sign of flamboyance to embark upon interpreting any biblical text, let alone one as contested as Galatians, without acknowledging the achievements of other interpreters, even those with whom one sometimes might disagree. Humility also induces one to enlist the help of one's colleagues, past and present, as often as one can. To ignore the many intellectual and cultural resources that have preceded one in any interpretive process is to destine one's work to a certain historical and cultural provincialism.

In this volume I have engaged and often depended upon the scholarly tradition, while simultaneously challenging it with my interpretation. Since I first began working seriously on this material ten years ago there have been significant developments in scholarship on both Galatians and the African American Christian traditions. I have attempted to reflect the various developments in contemporary scholarship in my documentation. Also, I have tried to refrain from placing excessive theoretical discussions in the body of the text and have located such discussions in the notes. The interested lay reader may find those discussions helpful. Additionally, I have translated all the Greek references for lay readers but allowed those Greek references to remain in the text for the benefit of my scholarly colleagues.

By training I am a scholar, and I would be delighted if my scholarly colleagues would engage this work, especially its unrelenting insistence on the importance of contemporary cultural frameworks for biblical interpretation. Yet the ultimate motivation of this volume is not that those in ivory towers would bless (or curse) this work, but that grassroots folk—a pastor, a deacon, a missionary, or a Sunday school teacher—might discover new ways of being both African American and Christian! If in a small way this volume liberates some saints on their way toward the kingdom, I will be satisfied.

1

Liberation and African American Experience

INTRODUCTION

*T*he race for African American liberation continues to be arduous. In many ways this quest has occupied the time and energy of my African American ancestors. From the first African presence in America to this very moment African Americans have traveled the long and stony road toward freedom. We have passed some hope-instilling landmarks along the way, but our ultimate destination still lies ahead.

Preceding generations of African Americans have run the race with dignity and courage. Today, in the opening years of the twenty-first century, African Americans who heroically marched through the civil rights revolution of the twentieth century are beginning to grow weary. They have handed the baton to a new generation, commanding us to run the next leg of the race. The exhortation in the book of Hebrews is pertinent for this present generation of African Americans: "Let *us* run with perseverance the race that is set before *us*." The old race now belongs to a new generation. Although we are surrounded by a great cloud of witnesses who cheer us on, it is now our responsibility to run.

With such a great responsibility it is incumbent upon this new generation not to run in vain, and so we must know why we are running. Certain people, looking at the burgeoning African American middle class[1] and the gains from the civil rights struggle, might conclude that the quest for African American liberation is no longer relevant. Then

1

there are others who see the effects of the bondage the African American community has suffered. These people intuitively know that liberation is needed, but they are paralyzed by the inability to define what liberation might mean in the context of modern African American life. Each group raises a very important question. For the first group the question is, "Why is liberation self-evidently necessary?" For the second group the question is, "What does liberation mean?"

LIBERATION: RATIONALES AND DEFINITIONS

In response to the first question there are abstract reasons one can offer for the necessity of liberation, but I offer a more common-sense reason that pulsates with the heartbeat of everyday African American life. Very simply, African Americans have seen the debilitating effects of bondage upon our collective self-esteem and our ability to be productive citizens. We know that such debilitation is contrary to the past greatness of persons of African descent and contrary to what we believe can be our future. African Americans have an existential rationale for the necessity of liberation.

We are separated from what we believe is our destiny, namely, to be leading and contributing citizens on a large scale. Much, but certainly not all of this separation is thought to be the result of the bondage African Americans have endured.[2] If an oppressor can shackle a people in chains and eradicate even the slightest remembrance of their former life of freedom and concomitantly assassinate their hope for future freedom, it may be possible to convince the oppressed that the chains around their wrists, ankles, and minds are natural. But if oppressed people hide even the most minute reminiscence of freedom in their hearts or have maintained even the smallest ability to imagine what freedom must be like, the chains for such people do not square existentially with their past or dreamt-for future.

One of my mentors, B. Herbert Martin,[3] who recently returned from Ghana in West Africa, provided a compelling example of the African ability to harbor hope for liberation even in the face of violent domination. In Ghana one of the time-honored crafts is stool-making. Craftspeople carve stools from wood, decorate them, and often present them as gifts. The importance of stool-making is related to the enormous significance of the "Golden Stool," a cultural artifact that represents for Ghanaians the spirit of the people and the abiding presence of the

Deity. One may liken the significance of the "Golden Stool" to that of the Ark of the Covenant for the Israelites. The "Golden Stool" is both a spiritual and a national symbol.

When the British set forth to colonize Ghana[4] their military objective was to "sit upon the Golden Stool," both literally and figuratively. If they accomplished this, the British felt that they would not only have captured the bodies of the Ghanaians, but would have decimated their souls as well.

In a decisive battle in 1900 the British did conquer the Ghanaians. Under the leadership of the Queen Mother of Ghana,[5] however, the Ghanaians, in a true spirit of "craftsmanship," manufactured a "pseudo Golden Stool" to serve as a surrogate, and they literally hid the real "Golden Stool." The British may have won that physical "battle," but since they did not truly sit upon *the* "Golden Stool" the Ghanaians had not lost the all-important "war." In their act of resistance the Ghanaians declared that they were "cast down, but not destroyed." African (American) people, who harbor this kind of indomitable hope in their bosoms, realize that the importance of liberation is not a matter of abstract reasoning, but of the inner spirit.

Scholars have documented extensively the insidious attempts to erase African American history from the records by historical lies and inaccuracies.[6] For example, addressing how slavery became institutionalized in antebellum America, Cheryl Kirk-Duggan writes:

> Manipulating texts, economics, ignorance, and fear sustained the American mutilation of African human beings. Just as Plato and Aristotle associated slavery with an idea of intelligent and virtuous superior authority ruling the world, many Western scholars used biological, biblical, religious, and philosophical doctrine to justify American slavery.[7]

In spite of these calculated efforts to suppress African American contributions there was enough strength in the voice of the African American oral tradition, and there were enough scholars to chronicle accurately the past glory of our African and African American forebears to mitigate the harsh results of these distortions. Moreover, there have been just enough African American educators, preachers, and public servants to inspire African Americans to imagine a world of thoroughgoing justice and equal opportunity.

A necessary (but not yet sufficient) number of African Americans know about a difficult but heroic past and can dream about a brighter future to keep liberation as a live option. Therefore we believe that the chains that have kept us from creating present greatness have to be broken. The importance of liberation, if one belongs to a dominant group, may need more abstract support, but if one belongs to a non-dominant group that is suffering from the effects of bondage the proof for the importance of liberation is an existential one. I remind the skeptics who remain unconvinced by my existential justification of the need for liberation that existential "diseases" often exhibit concrete symptoms. The mistake people make when engaging in emancipation projects is that they frequently treat the symptoms without seeking cures for the "diseases." A personal anecdote may further clarify this point.

Before taking my current position as a divinity school professor I served for five years as the senior pastor of a middle-class, interdenominational African American church in an impoverished neighborhood in Baltimore, Maryland. One summer Saturday I joined men from our congregation in a neighborhood cleanup. As I swept up hundreds of pieces of broken glass and other carelessly discarded rubbish that morning, I realized that the sordid alleys of the neighborhood did not look this way simply because people were "trifling." Each piece of broken glass represented some aspect of "brokenness" in the lives of many of this neighborhood's residents.

Honestly, some of this "brokenness" was self-inflicted, the outworking of the compounded effects of poor personal decision-making. Yet much of this "brokenness" was the tragic result of persons being heirs of "transgenerational suffering."[8] In America racism, sexism, and classism mutually reinforce each other in such complex ways that it is possible for a (black) family, whether in an urban or rural context, to pass on its "legacy" of poverty (both of resources and of spirit) in the same way that many well-to-do (white) families have bequeathed their legacy of wealth. Regardless of the different origins of the "brokenness" I witnessed that Saturday morning, it was obvious to me that until we "cleaned up" some larger issues of alienation and rage in that community our sweeping of broken glass was a futile enterprise.

Cornel West has perceptively recognized the existential origins of the contemporary black dilemma. West has called for "a direct attack on the sense of worthlessness and self-loathing in black America."[9] He further observes:

> Black existential *angst* derives from the lived experiences of ontological
> wounds and emotional scars inflicted by white supremacist beliefs and

images permeating U.S. society and culture. . . . The accumulated effect of the black wounds and scars suffered in a white-dominated society is a deep-seated anger, a boiling sense of rage, and a passionate pessimism regarding America's will to justice.[10]

In short, since the current dilemmas that assail African Americans have profound existential dimensions, solutions that seek to alleviate the dilemmas must acknowledge and speak to those existential dimensions.

In consideration of the second question ("What does liberation mean?") let me acknowledge from the outset that I have severe misgivings about my attempt to define liberation too carefully. Anyone familiar with African American culture knows that African Americans are poetic people for whom exactness is not at all times a virtue. Some examples might elucidate this fascinating cultural point.

I am blessed to have as friends several gifted African American gospel and jazz vocalists and musicians. These friends have taught me that much of the strength and resonance of African American vocalists lies in their ability not simply to hit a musical note exactly, but to move around the "margins" of a note, thereby increasing the vibrato and resonance of the sound.

When, for example, Kathleen Battle, the celebrated African American opera singer, performs European musical works, she adds enormous texture to those works by powerful yet playful vocal variations on a note. Musical technicians might refer to this is "coloratura." As this technical term suggests, the vocal variation adds enormous "color" to the presentation. When one too precisely hits a note or too accurately defines a reality in black and white, some of the color that captivates and motivates may be lost. This is enough of an excursus into the world of music. Theology also offers us insights into the African American wariness of an overemphasis on precision at all costs.

Eugene Genovese gives an example of how this African American wariness concerning precision manifested itself theologically in the American slave era. African Americans in slavery had no problems in their sermons and religious testimonies conflating the roles of Moses and Jesus. What was important to them was not the accurate placement of Moses in 1450 B.C.E. or of Jesus in 30 C.E., but rather the poetic power emanating from the narrative accounts of the liberating activities of these individuals.[11] My hesitation at suggesting too specifically what liberation might mean stems from the fear of committing what African Americans might call "the heresy of exactness."

Later I will discuss the particular ways in which African Americans
have defined their existence in America socially. In the final analysis, regardless of economic status or educational achievement, the social factor
that arguably has most defined and shaped the existence of African
Americans is *blackness.*

Even as I assert the importance of blackness I am fully aware that
race, gender, class, and sexual orientation combine in sundry and complex ways to legitimate the power of those who already have power and
to deny access to power to those who are on the margins. For example,
the womanist movement[12] began in part because of black male theologians' unwillingness to acknowledge that black women's oppression re-
sulted not simply from white racism, but also from the sexism that was
(and still is) rampant in black culture. On the other hand, womanist
thinkers have contended that their white feminist counterparts have
rightly acknowledged the oppressive realities of patriarchy. But many of
these white feminists have been reluctant to address the oppressive role
of white racism.

Though I focus on blackness in this present discussion, I am mind-
ful of the wisdom of Patricia Hill Collins. Collins has advocated the
need for a paradigm shift in our discussion of domination and resistance. She has encouraged us to view issues of race, gender, class, sexual
orientation, and religion as factors that can contribute to a structure of
domination.[13] These caveats will be borne in mind as this discussion
proceeds. Since the concept of blackness figures prominently in my
definition of liberation, I shall discuss what I mean by it in this context.

BLACKNESS:
BIOLOGY AND IDEOLOGY

In this book when I refer to blackness in the African American context I am not only interested in the biological features that distinguish
people of African descent (e.g., skin color, texture of hair, and facial features). In terms of biology, one does not choose to be black. This is pre-
determined at the moment of conception. In addition to biological
matters, when I speak about blackness I mean above all the constant
and difficult choice to be consciously black and to accept as part of one's
identity the history, joys, and struggles of black people. What has constituted this conscious choice throughout African Americans' quest for
liberation has varied depending upon the circumstances, but often it
has meant the proud acknowledgment and acceptance of these biologi-

cal features as they have been part and parcel of our history, joys, and struggles.

In this characterization it is possible for one to be black biologically but not *black* in the ideological sense. Also, it is possible for one who is white biologically to sympathize with the African American struggle, but only up to a point, for the possibility always remains for a white person to stop "being black" at any moment that the struggles of being black no longer fit that person's agenda.

There are notable examples of sympathetic white persons who want to "be black." In an ironic twist of history one witnesses, for example, many white teenagers in the United States emulating the heroes and heroines of black popular culture, especially the superstars of the rap music industry. The "crossover" appeal of rap artists such as Tupac Shakur and Lil' Kim among white youth indicates that "being black" is seen as desirable up to a point. White culture has never had any difficulty conceding various aspects of the entertainment industry to black persons.

Many African Americans have failed to see how the entertainment industry in certain instances continues to be a mechanism of white economic exploitation. In a market culture it is permissible for white persons to want to "be black" as long as blackness is associated with a style of dress and a particular kind of music.[14] Rarely in such a market culture does one see blackness being associated with values and realities such as self-determination, political mobilization, and high economic and intellectual achievement.

My contention that sympathetic white persons can only "be black" to a certain point necessitates a further statement about the interesting interplay of biology and ideology[15] in the construction of blackness as an identity. Over the last several decades there has been robust discussion among social scientists and cultural critics concerning the constituent features of a racial or ethnic identity.[16]

Attempting to ascertain the features that constitute one's "race," many contemporary social scientists are quick to assert that race is not so much biologically determined as it is socially constructed. In other words, communities and cultural systems assign values and establish hierarchies for groups of people according to differences in physiognomy. The biological differences exist, but genetically such differences are "neutral." Whether these "neutral" physical differences receive positive or negative valences is determined by various cultural forces at work in any society.[17]

Social science's current emphasis on the role that culture plays in establishing one's racial identity is, in part, an important corrective to the unjust, even pernicious "scientific racism" of the last three centuries. Convinced that the white race was genetically superior, countless white "scientists" set out to prove, for example, that the skulls of white persons were larger than those of blacks. These "scientists" then extrapolated from these spurious statistics theories asserting that white people were genetically superior to black people because their larger skulls implied greater mental capacity.[18]

In an effort to counteract the adverse effects of scientific racism other scholars, such as the celebrated German-Jewish cultural anthropologist Franz Boas,[19] began to offer strong counterarguments to the supposed biological inferiority of the black race. Boas contended that the claims of black inferiority would be impossible to maintain if and when scientists would investigate the monumental contributions of African persons to world civilization. In the face of racist claims of biological inferiority certain scholars affirmed that persons with black skin had made as many contributions to the forward progress of human civilizations as any other group of people, and perhaps even more.

Social science's highlighting of the role of culture in creating racial identity helps to account for the fluidity and even ambiguity that sometimes exists when one attempts to define or describe racial characteristics. It is impossible to predict how *all* people who are "black," "brown," "white," or "yellow" will act simply based on the biological features they share. Such essentialist claims flatly deny the enormous influence that geography, family upbringing, religious instruction, and cultural institutions exert on personal behavior and preferences.

Yet one must be careful not to take the corrective insights about the social construction of racial identity to a logical extreme. While it is profitable to remove oppressive hierarchies from the physiological differences that occur among various racial groups, one should not ignore that these physiological differences do exist. To assert that blackness is simply a state of mind or an ideological commitment is to engage in a dangerous revisionist history that turns a blind eye to the role that skin color, facial features, and hair texture have played in the domination of black people.

Likewise, any ideology or interpretive strategy that ignores the physical dimensions of blackness dishonors the legacy of the African ancestors in this country who paid for our present existence not simply with their black souls, but also with their black bodies. The cautionary note of Michael

Omi and Howard Winant is well-taken. They write: "There is a continuous temptation to think of race as an essence, as something fixed, concrete and objective. . . . And there is also an opposite temptation to see it as a mere illusion, which an ideal social order would eliminate."[20]

There *was* nothing illusionary or abstract about slave owners whipping and raping their slaves. There *is* nothing illusionary or abstract about "the look" of amazement, surprise, and scorn that black people receive when they walk into certain professional and social gatherings, which historically have been attended solely by white people. There are things in a "politically correct" world that certain polite white people would never say with their mouths. Yet occasionally those white people are unable to censor their eyes. Their eyes raise the question, "What are *you* doing here?"—"you" meaning "you black person."

As a black person, when I receive "the look" from a white person I know that blackness is more than an *attitude*. Blackness, whether it is frowned upon by prejudiced persons or celebrated by the children of Africa, does have *corporeal* aspects to it. Commenting on how the physical aspects of blackness should and do participate prominently in the creation of black identity, Michael Dyson poignantly observes:

> As the old saying goes, you can tell the policeman that race is a trope, but if he is beating your head and you're saying, "Listen, this is a historically constituted, socially constructed reality that has no basis beyond our agreement and consensus in American culture," that's cool, but your head is still being beaten. So the material consequences of the association of race with black identity, with black skin, has to be acknowledged as a serious consequence against which we must articulate our understanding.[21]

Historically, in many instances dominant white American culture used the notion of blackness to build a society upon the rhetoric of democracy and the beaten backs of slaves thought to be inferior because of their darker skins. African Americans have taken the same concept of blackness, however, and have used it as a tool to build a distinctive culture, which is both *black* and American.[22] Thus African Americans have learned to use blackness as a rallying point and as a hallmark of our existence.[23]

If I were to frame my understanding of blackness in biblical terms I might contend that African Americans have taken the stone that the builders rejected—the physical traits despised by the dominant culture—and made them the cornerstone.[24] Just as Christians celebrate the very reality that disqualified Jesus from being the messiah in the eyes of some, namely his ignominious execution,[25] so too African Americans must continually appreciate the physical aspects of our blackness.

If in our philosophical machinations we devise ways of being black that categorically eschew the affirmation of the distinct biological traits associated with people of African descent we unwittingly perpetuate the dangerous dualism that separates body and soul. Such dualism impugns the radical message of the Incarnation, which asserts that God is so concerned about human particularity that God decided to enrobe God's own self in human particularity. Womanist theologian Kelly Brown Douglas has powerfully advocated the need for the understanding of black identity to include robust affirmations of black bodies. Douglas writes:

> White cultural attacks have infringed upon black women's and men's appreciation for their own embodied black selves. White culture has systematically and unrelentingly cast aspersions upon Black physiognomy: hair, skin color, facial features, genitals. This culture has decried blackness as ugly and evil. Unfortunately, too many black men and women have internalized this profane spiritual discourse of white culture. In so doing, they have been unable to authentically love their own bodies. So while black people may verbalize their love of God, their lack of self-love suggests otherwise. A love of one's own body is a fundamental component to saying a loud yes to God's profound and gracious (meaning freely given) love. The radicality of God's love expressed in Jesus Christ means that God loves our very bodies.[26]

For the reasons cogently expressed above by Brown Douglas, I am hesitant to understand blackness as simply a social construction or an ideological position. In light of this, the liberation so sorely needed in the African American community must empower black people to feel comfortable about the cultural and physical characteristics that create our blackness. Additionally, liberation will foster among black people a celebration of our bodies as loci of the creative genius of God who loves particularity and difference.

Hopefully, this detailed discussion has demonstrated that any liberation effort must address both physiological and ideological dimensions. Yet as we seek freedom in these dimensions African Americans must always be on guard, lest our construal of the freedom project become narcissistic. The goal is not simply that I love my black self, but that by loving my black self I am set free to more fully care for and love other selves, especially other black selves.

In her classic definition of the womanist, Alice Walker advocates the need for holistic love and concern among black people. Walker writes, "[The womanist] loves music. Loves dance. Loves the moon. *Loves* the Spirit. Loves love and food and roundness. Loves struggle. *Loves* the Folk. Loves herself. Regardless."[27] This insistence on the need to love "the folk" must stay at the center of our discussions about liberation. Gaining personal fulfillment is an important feature of liberation, but efforts for emancipation must equally emphasize communal aspects as well.

Along the way, authentic liberation will bring about profound changes in the personal lives of African Americans. Yet because of the emphasis in African American culture on community and group membership and the significance that is placed upon race in America, liberation cannot simply mean the freedom for individual African Americans to do their own thing for their own material benefit. Peter Paris observes: "It should not be surprising to discover that the African American understanding of personhood is integrally related to the communal struggle for racial justice. That quest is deeply rooted in the African experience of tribal community, the basic condition for familial and individual life."[28]

Liberation, in its fullest expression, for African Americans will promote personal fulfillment and at the same time sponsor efforts for larger social uplift. Unless this personal transformation is accompanied by a social transformation[29] the liberation effort may become a crass affair of the survival of the fittest and a demonstration of unchecked individualism. Or to put that in the African American vernacular, unless liberation efforts push for socio-political as well as personal freedoms African Americans will be beset with a "job-Saab" mentality: as long as I have a job and am driving a Saab, then there is no racism, sexism, homophobia, poverty, and self-hate in the African American community. Liberation cannot simply mean the material success of a few individuals.

I have argued that liberation in the African American context will have a decided social aspect. A very important function of a society or community is the creation and perpetuation of its ideology. I believe that it is precisely at the ideological level where the African American intellectual[30] generally, and the African American biblical scholar particularly, can make great contributions to the liberation effort.

Just as there are and should be economic and political aspects to the African American quest for liberation, there must also be ideological aspects. Even though African Americans no longer wear the physical

shackles of slavery, we in many instances are still bound by the dominant white culture's ideology and portrayal of African Americans. There
is a relationship between the dominant ideology and the dominant
ideology's portrayal of African American culture.

White depiction of African American life and culture has been both
pervasive and perverse. One can search anything, from medical records
to Hollywood movies, to see what the dominant culture has believed
about African Americans.[31] Because African Americans were thought to
be subhuman it seemed "natural" to use us as guinea pigs for all kinds of
medical experiments. Because African Americans were thought to be
shiftless, we have consistently been depicted by the media as a race of
people who are drug dealers, pimps, and welfare recipients. African
Americans have continually received the message that our culture is
reprobate. Overwhelmed by that message, some have been led to believe
that the only valuable culture is white American culture. Thus some
African Americans have assimilated to that culture, and many of those
who have held on to African American culture have done so with a
sense of inadequacy.

If the contribution of African Americans to America is to be adequately recognized, and if the beauty and brilliance of African American culture is to be appreciated fully, African Americans must take
responsibility for valuing our own lives and depicting our own culture
and ideologies. Many societies build their identity and ideologies upon
the charter documents of that society. America is no different in this regard. Here the charter documents include the Declaration of Independence, the Constitution, and the Bible. Therefore, given the foundational
importance of the Bible in American society, as African Americans
strive to depict our culture and articulate our ideologies we must seize
hermeneutical control in our use of the Bible.[32]

AFRICAN AMERICAN BIBLICAL INTERPRETATION

When studying the Bible we must bring African American life and
culture to bear on our interpretive efforts. If we fail to do so, white society
will continue to shape the world of the African American in a white
image. This will no longer do. Thus, of the many things that liberation
may mean in the modern African American context, it surely means the
ability to create and shape our world in our image and to tell our story
for ourselves. A liberating African American hermeneutic[33] strives for
this end. Before I set forth the methodology of this hermeneutic, a dis-

cussion of some of the historical currents, values, and presuppositions that have shaped African American experience and thought will prove helpful. I need, however, to make one qualification.

This hermeneutic is more precisely an African American Christian hermeneutic. As I discuss its historical roots I am specifically interested in how African American Christians have engaged with the Bible. Given the increased religious diversity among African Americans[34] I, as a Christian interpreter, readily acknowledge that our efforts for liberation will, of necessity, traverse religious barriers.

There are obviously significant segments of the African American population who are not Christian. More work needs to be done in relating the liberation hermeneutics of African American Christianity with, for instance, the liberation hermeneutics of African Americans who are members of the Nation of Islam or Muslim communities.[35] The liberation effort will require a concerted response from all facets of African American culture. My exploration targets what African American Christians can do to aid the cause.

By no means does one necessarily have to possess Christian commitments to employ the strategies and insights of the hermeneutic that I will assert. I believe that the reading I offer will espouse some principles that have come from African American Christian experience and others emanating from general African American experience. Thus the interpretive yield of this hermeneutic may be attractive to people regardless of their religious affiliations or lack thereof. By calling it a Christian hermeneutic I am saying that this hermeneutic's major architects have been, and are, members of the African American Christian community and that this hermeneutic's primary, but certainly not exclusive, audience also will be African American Christians.

First, in African American (Christian) culture, the importance of community and social experience cannot be overemphasized. Historically, African American Christians have defined themselves socially and not doctrinally. What has bound us together is not so much strict adherence to confessions or creeds but rather the common joys and woes associated with having dark skin in a country that worships whiteness. Vincent Wimbush writes: "They [Afro-Christian communities] understood and explained their existence not through exclusive theological propositions or dogma, but chiefly on account of social—here including political and economic and educational—realities."[36]

In spite of the slave traders' merciless practice of separating African families in order to quell the threat of slave revolt, Africans who were brought to the United States in the slave trade were able to carve out a cultural identity. Since they were often without the essential building block of the biological family, how were they able to accomplish this?

One possible explanation is that Americans of African descent found a new societal building block, African American Christianity and the African American church.[37] It could be argued that these served to supply many with a surrogate family. In this surrogate family, the Bible was not a book from which to extract doctrine but rather a source of information teaching the slaves how to comport themselves toward each other and their white counterparts. Contrasting the use of the Bible in certain segments of white and black culture, Eugene Genovese writes: "For the Blacks the Bible provides an inexhaustible store of good advice for a proper life; it does not usually provide an unchanging body of doctrine as with white fundamentalists."[38]

The slaves transformed the book religion of the Europeans and slave-holders into meaningful commentaries on their own social experience.[39] Their interpretations did not rest with the simple exposition of what had happened in a biblical story. They used biblical stories to illumine what their social experience was, and hopefully would be. Thus they interpreted their social experience in terms of the Bible. The biblical stories and passages that most often attracted them were those dealing with liberation and equality, two things that they desperately wanted. But were these African American interpretations any different from those of the slaveholders?

Those who are unfamiliar with the distinctiveness of African American culture might suggest that the biblical readings of the slaves naturally followed the ideology of the oppressors, and thereby the liberating value of these readings obviously was tainted by the dominant ideology. Such a suggestion, although inaccurate, allows me to give nuance to the interaction between the dominant ideology and the African American liberation effort.

Historically the large African American presence in the United States had its genesis in the iniquitous institution of American slavery, which was buttressed by a hegemonic ideology. In that regard African Americans have, in some sense, always begun with the dominant ideology, but not remained beholden to it. The genius of African Americans has been our ability to carve roads of cultural identity through the mountains of the racist ideology of the dominant society, thereby transforming opposition into opportunities for cultural distinctiveness. With respect to the slaves' transformation of dominant white Christianity, Genovese wonderfully captures the genius of the African spirit that yet lingers in the African American psyche. He remarks:

> Traditional West African religions did not espouse a doctrine of original sin, and the acceptance of Christianity by African peoples never did result in a full surrender to this most profound and fateful of Christian ideas. The idea of original sin lies at the heart of the Western formulation of the problem of freedom and order. In time it tipped the ideological scales decisively toward the side of individual freedom in its perpetual struggle with the demands for social order. For the West Africans the scales remained tipped toward social order so long as their world-view and the social basis on which it rested remained traditional. . . . The slaves reshaped the Christianity they had embraced; they conquered the religion of those who had conquered them. . . . The slaves developed an Afro-American and Christian humanism that affirmed joy in life in the face of every trial.[40]

Abstract, doctrinal readings of Scripture that have little or nothing to do with the pulse of life have never been characteristic of an African American appropriation of Scripture. The very existence of the African American church proves this. The exodus of black Christians from white churches to form their own churches was primarily prompted by social and cultural forces. Eugene Genovese writes: "For the Blacks the move to separate was thus both a positive desire for independent cultural expression and a defense against racism. . . . [the] separation helped them to widen the degree of autonomy they were steadily carving out of their oppressors' regime."[41]

An African American interpretation of Scripture has been and should be guided by social realities. If the Bible is to have any sway in the African American community it must speak to communal as well as personal needs; it must address social as well as psychological problems.

African Americans should also attempt to eschew ruling class ideologies. Itumeleng Mosala has issued a clarion call to all who are interested in doing liberation hermeneutics. He writes:

> Existential commitments to the liberation struggles of the oppressed are inadequate because those who are committed in this way are often still ideologically and theoretically enslaved to the dominant discourses in the society. . . . A clear ideological and theoretical break with the dominant practices and discourses is necessary if a biblical hermeneutics of black liberation is to emerge.[42]

In support of Mosala's claim, the painful realities of slavery, overt segregation, and now the subtle, sophisticated racism[43] of the twenty-first century have demonstrated the horrors often associated with ruling-class ideologies. A liberating African American hermeneutic and ideology desire not to get the upper hand on white people and usurp their position as a ruling class, making them the dominated. Certainly these strands of thinking have existed in various segments of the African American community, but revenge or a switching of the poles between dominant and dominated is not the goal.

The persistent quest for freedom in America has taught African Americans the very valuable lesson that ruling class discourses not only oppress the oppressed, but they also oppress the oppressors. Slaveholders looked upon African Americans as less than human. According to the United States Constitution an African American was only three-fifths of a person. The ruling class ideology, which supported slavery, had blinded white Americans to the humanity of African Americans.

The slaves' humanity was real. Yet a ruling class discourse had prevented many white Americans from seeing this reality. The inability to perceive reality accurately, or what the Marxists might call "false-consciousness," is a form of oppression. Recognizing that a ruling-class ideology enslaves both the oppressor and the oppressed, an African American hermeneutic cannot adopt such an ideology or allow it to go unchecked. The sentiments of George Fitzhugh, a Virginia slaveowner in 1854, indicate how blinding a ruling class ideology can be. Fitzhugh remarked: "Some men are born with saddles on their backs, and others booted and spurred to ride them, and the riding does them good."[44]

Martin Luther King, Jr. spoke poignantly about the injurious effects of hate upon the one who hates. King remarked: "Hate destroys a man's sense of values and his objectivity. It causes him to describe the beautiful as ugly and the ugly as beautiful, and to confuse the true with the false and the false with the true."[45] If we simply substitute the words "ruling class ideology" for the word "hate," King's comments could apply to the injurious and oppressive effects of a ruling class ideology upon the minds of the ruling class. A ruling class ideology impairs one's ability to accurately perceive reality.

A liberating African American hermeneutic is not comfortable with a "master-servant" relationship in the world of interpretation, even if by some coup or whim of fate African Americans were to become the "masters." Once again the historical experience of African Americans provides insight into the self-understanding of this hermeneutic.

Throughout the struggle to overcome racism in all its ugly manifestations African Americans, in the main, have sought not so much to deny or denigrate the humanity of white people as to affirm our own African American humanity. Our quest is not so much for revenge as it is for recognition.

Readings of Scripture that take African American experience seriously are not purposed to slay white hegemonic interpretations on the altar of cultural pluralism for all of their past atrocities. Instead, by articulating their self-understanding and goals African American engagements with the Bible hope to offer themselves as interpretive possibilities for people who are uninspired or not helped by traditional white or Eurocentric interpretations, with their proclivity to lock textual meaning in the prison of the past. The point is that liberating African American readings of the Bible are not seeking to overthrow the interpretive world by means of a black power regime. Rather, these interpretations hope to gain respect and equality as interpretive possibilities. Recognition is the goal.

Recognition by whom? By the larger non-black world of scholars and lay people alike. For centuries African Americans have known about our liberating ways of reading the Bible. Our presence today as a people, in spite of all the forces that have contested our existence, is a testimony to our liberating engagements with the Bible. Yet, due to the large role of oral tradition in our culture and the disturbing lack of African American presence in higher education, the brilliant gems of interpretive wisdom from our community have not been displayed to large audiences. An African American hermeneutic is in some ways successful if it polishes the collective interpretive wisdom of African Americans and displays it for large audiences who may not like what they see but hopefully will at least respect and appreciate it.

Literary critic Stanley Fish, whose work I will discuss in Chapter Two, has provided us with a useful and intriguing "acid test" for the viability of a mode of thought. Fish writes:

> The true power of a form of inquiry or thought . . . [can be seen] when the assumptions encoded in the vocabulary of a form of thought become inescapable in the larger society. For example, people who have never read a feminist tract and would be alarmed at the thought of reading one are nevertheless being influenced by feminist thinking in ways of which they are unaware or are to some extent uncomfortably aware. Such influence often exhibits itself in the form of resistance: "I'm not going to fall in with any of that feminist crap," thereby falling in headfirst as it were.[46]

Stanley Fish helps us to see that resistance is a form of recognition, and even respect. Thus even if critics are not ultimately persuaded by the readings that an African American hermeneutic produces, the fact that traditional biblical critics must now contend with such readings is an important advancement in the African American quest for liberation.[47]

A liberating African American hermeneutic should not covet the oppressive title of "the proper interpretation of the text;" it merely wants its validity to be recognized so that it can take its rightful place alongside other interpretive models and create a dialogue among equals. This hermeneutic is happy just being one interpretive possibility among many, but it is an interpretive possibility that continually challenges other interpretations to be socially relevant for contemporary life.[48]

As I hope the above discussion has indicated, many features characterize the sophistication and complexity of African American life, but one of its most salient features is that of tension: the tension born of an ambiguous existence. From our initial presence in the United States onwards, African Americans have felt the tension associated with holding on to an African heritage while trying relentlessly to build an American identity.

This tension born out of living between two continents obviously has roots in the slave era of American history. Many minority groups from other continents who have come to America have experienced the tension. But I contend that, if not unique, certainly the African American variety of this tension is highly unusual because of the manner in which my ancestors were brought to the United States and the reception they received upon their arrival. Here is where similarities among African Americans and other immigrant groups begin to break down.

Noting how Europeans who fled to America were amalgamated into mainstream (read here "white") culture, James Baldwin remarked:

> They [European immigrants] come through Ellis Island, where *Giorgio* becomes *Joe, Pappavasiliu* becomes *Palmer, Evangelos* becomes *Evans, Goldsmith* becomes *Smith* or *Gold,* and *Avakian* becomes *King.* So, with a painless change of name, and in the twinkling of an eye, one becomes a white American. . . . The Irish middle passage, for but one example, was as foul as my own, and as dishonorable on the part of those responsible for it. But the Irish became white when they got here and began rising in the world, whereas I became black and began sinking.[49]

My African ancestors did not come to America with hopes and visions of a better existence. They were victims of a crime. Genovese writes: "The reception accorded by white Americans to the black people brought here [America] in chains and raised in slavery . . . has provided a record of one of history's greatest crimes."[50]

The slave traders would begin the process of "de-Africanizing" the slaves almost immediately upon procuring the Africans. I heard stories of this in the spring of 1992 when I traveled to the Gambia in West Africa. The Gambians told me how the enslavers, when taking the Gambians from the coastal lands for transport to Britain and America, would take from the necks of the Africans the colorful beads they wore and used as money. The slave traders did this to strip the Gambians of their former culture and homeland. These traders knew that there was a positive correlation between a people's history and its hope. Thus they tried to abolish the Africans' sense of history.

Moreover, Africans in America needed not think even for a moment that they were Americans. The beatings, lynchings, and the psychological demoralization of having to call someone "master" experientially told them that they were not Americans. They were not allowed to be Africans, and they were not accepted as Americans. The continual denial of full citizenship for African Americans has persisted long after the demise of chattel slavery. James Baldwin sagaciously explored the irony and ambiguity of twentieth-century African Americans fighting abroad in the American armed forces for a freedom that was not even afforded them in their own country. Baldwin wrote: "The romance of treason never occurred to us [African American soldiers] for the brutally simple reason that you can't betray a country you don't have. . . . Treason draws its energy from the conscious, deliberate betrayal of a trust—as we were not trusted, we could not betray. And we did not wish to be traitors. We wished to be citizens."[51] The ambiguity of being stripped of one identity and never fully afforded another has been sufficient enough to create existential tension in African Americans.

Throughout our history African Americans have experienced forces that have tried to divide our identity. W. E. B. Du Bois masterfully captured this ambiguity of the divided identity. Du Bois remarked:

> Here, then is the dilemma, and it is a puzzling one, I admit. No Negro who has given earnest thought to the situation of his people in America has failed, at some time in life, to find himself at these crossroads; has failed to ask himself at some time: what, after all, am I? Am I an American or am I a Negro? Can I be both?[52]

Du Bois would also write: "One ever feels his twoness—an American, a Negro; two souls, two thoughts, two unreconciled strivings; two warring ideals in one dark body, whose dogged strength alone keeps it from being torn asunder."[53]

I contend that one of the virtues of African Americans has been our ability to hold the warring ideals of which Du Bois spoke in a dialectical tension and to allow this tension to define and energize our lives. The truth of our existence is this tension. Even though this ambiguity was cast upon us by others, African Americans have transformed this tension of ambiguity into a hallmark of our existence. Moreover, African Americans know that to resolve the tension is to suck the life-blood out of our culture and to obliterate our identity.

Forces have tried to strip African Americans of an identity by prohibiting us from being either African or American. We, by means of creativity, imagination, and resistance, have carved out our identity by declaring that we are both African and American. Thus African American life is the tension between these two warring ideals and the struggle to prohibit external forces from resolving the tension; the tension is our identity.

In the American context, in spite of many gains in civil and human rights, race is still arguably the deciding factor. The record is full of African Americans who have risen to levels of economic and social prominence but who are still reminded by "the powers that be" that black skin, even when it possesses green money, is still only second best. Yet, historically, African Americans have celebrated our black skins and black culture. And herein lies the struggle. African Americans have desired to count as a blessing what the dominant culture wants to curse as our bane.

African Americans will use this struggle to provide the context for a contemporary reading of Scripture. If, in fact, this hermeneutic is interested not so much in interpreting the Bible as it is in interpreting life in terms of the Bible, and if life in America is defined above all things else by race and the struggles associated with race, then one of the many questions an African American hermeneutic will ask of texts will be this: "How does this text speak directly or indirectly to the struggle of being black in America?"

As we struggle to demand our American rights and to affirm our African heritage, and as we struggle to love about ourselves the very thing that has caused us to be hated, what positive or negative lessons can African Americans learn from a text, and what lessons can we teach a text? Being black in America is an ongoing struggle for African Americans that cuts across social and economic class. For this reason, that struggle must serve as a rallying point in the quest for liberation.

NOTES: CHAPTER 1

[1] For a recent and helpful discussion of the rise of the black middle class see Marvin A. McMickle, *Preaching to the Black Middle Class: Words of Challenge, Words of Hope* (Valley Forge, Pa.: Judson Press, 2000) 1–16.

[2] In this book I speak forcefully about the enduring effects of white domination upon African American people and culture. Yet as I evaluate the current problems in the African American community I must also assert that not all the pathology in the African American community emanates from white domination and "the slavery plantation." In other words, a strident assessment of the effects of white domination does not absolve one from turning a critical gaze upon African American culpability and irresponsibility.

[3] B. Herbert Martin is the pastor of the Progressive Community Center: The People's Church, on the south side of Chicago. Through his leadership this church has become a vibrant force in social empowerment and racial reconciliation in Chicago.

[4] From approximately 1880 to 1905 the French and British colonized most of West Africa. Prior to this formal political colonization European nations had been importing slaves from Africa for three hundred years. For a useful history of the European slave trade and of the colonization of West Africa see Michael Crowder, *West Africa: An Introduction to its History* (London: Longman, 1977).

[5] Ibid. 140–41.

[6] Jeremiah Wright forthrightly addresses the lies white culture has perpetuated about black culture. Wright remarks, "Most African Americans have heard the lie that Black people don't really have a culture. Most of us have been told that if it had not been for Europeans capturing some of us, bringing us to America, teaching us a few things, colonizing our extended families in Africa, and teaching them a few things, to this day we would still have no culture. . . . Of course, not all Africans and African Americans have accepted these lies as truth. . . . Some African American scholars have uncovered evidence that, contrary to popular belief, the opposite of the traditional lies is true. They discovered that if it had not been for Africans, perhaps Europeans would not have had any culture at all, for they got most of the original civilizing information from us, not the other way around." See Wright, *Africans Who Shaped Our Faith* (Chicago: Urban Ministries, 1995) 19.

[7] Cheryl A. Kirk-Duggan, *Exorcizing Evil: A Womanist Perspective on the Spirituals* (Maryknoll, N.Y.: Orbis, 1997) 22.

[8] For a discussion of the "transgenerational" character of black suffering see Clarice J. Martin, "Biblical Theodicy and Black Women's Spiritual Autobiography," in Emilie M. Townes, ed., *A Troubling In My Soul: Womanist Perspectives on Evil and Suffering* (Maryknoll, N.Y.: Orbis, 1993) 22–23. Martin's discussion

is predicated upon the earlier study of Black suffering by William R. Jones, "Theodicy: The Controlling Category for Black Theology," *The Journal of Religious Thought* 30 (1973) 28–38.

[9] Cornel West, *Race Matters* (Boston: Beacon, 1993) 17.

[10] Ibid. 17–18.

[11] Eugene Genovese, *Roll Jordan Roll: The World the Slaves Made* (New York: Vintage Books, 1974) 253.

[12] The womanist movement articulates the specific opportunities and challenges of black women.

[13] See Patricia Hill Collins, *Black Feminist Thought: Knowledge, Consciousness, and the Politics of Empowerment* (New York: Routledge, 1990) 222–30. In this book my emphasis on racial/ethnic realities is not an attempt to ignore the other factors that comprise one's social identity. Rather, I contend that when we bring the discussion of racial/ethnic identity into sharp focus, fascinating analogues and even parallels between the ancient world of Galatia and the contemporary world of African Americans may emerge. In the history of Galatians scholarship there has been a tendency to downplay the ethnic implications of the controversy between the Jewish Christians and the Gentile Christians in that ancient community. In the American context, there has been a tendency to evade serious discussions about the thoroughgoing role that race and ethnicity have played, and continue to play, in every aspect of American culture.

[14] For a provocative analysis of how black entertainers (especially rap artists) either contribute to or destroy various racial stereotypes see Michael Eric Dyson, "Gangsta Rap and American Culture," in his *Between God and Gangsta Rap: Bearing Witness to Black Culture* (New York: Oxford University Press, 1996) 176–86.

[15] In this book the term "ideology" will have several general meanings that will be made clear by the context. According to Terry Eagleton, ideology in its more neutral sense refers to "a body of ideas characteristic of a particular social group or class," and also to "the promotion and legitimation of the interests of such social groups in the face of opposing groups," and these interests will have "some relevance to the sustaining or challenging of a whole political way of life." See Eagleton, *Ideology* (London: Verso, 1991) 1, 29. When used in its more pejorative sense, with respect to white American society, (dominant) ideology will refer to "ideas and beliefs which help to legitimate the interests of a ruling group or class specifically by distortion or dissimulation" (ibid. 30). With respect to the text of Galatians, (dominant) ideology will refer to ideas of the conservative Jewish Christian wing, which certainly was not a ruling group in the larger socio-political world of Roman imperialism. Nevertheless, this conservative Jewish Christian wing did wield power within early Christianity.

[16] I do not draw a sharp distinction between the terms "race" and "ethnicity." In this book both terms are used to suggest the powerful drive in people to

draw boundaries, real or perceived, around themselves. It is more appropriate, however, to speak of "ethnicity" than of "race" in the ancient biblical context, since biblical peoples seemed less aware of physical (and especially color) differences among people. In the contemporary American context, even though we know that biological differences are "neutral," these differences continue to play decisive cultural and political roles. Thus to draw too sharp a distinction between "race" (i.e., biological differences) and "ethnicity" (i.e., cultural differences) may obscure how intertwined these are in America. For recent studies that argue that "race" is a useless category see Dave Unander, *Shattering the Myth of Race: Genetic Realities and Biblical Truths* (Valley Forge, Pa.: Judson Press, 2000), and Hope Landrine and Elizabeth A. Klonoff, *African American Acculturation: Deconstructing Race and Reviving Culture* (Thousand Oaks, Calif.: Sage Publications, 1996).

[17] A.K.M. Adam remarks: "Identity . . . is constructed when people decide that certain distinctions make a difference and others do not." See his *What is Postmodern Biblical Criticism?* (Minneapolis: Fortress, 1995) 29.

[18] For a discussion of "scientific" attempts to prove the inferiority of African Americans see, for example, Alessandra Lorini, *Rituals of Race: American Public Culture and the Search for Racial Democracy* (Charlottesville: University Press of Virginia, 1999) 82–83. Also see Michael Omi and Howard Winant, "Racial Formations," in Paula S. Rothenberg, ed., *Race, Class, and Gender in the United States: An Integrated Study* (New York: St. Martin's Press, 1998) 14.

[19] I specifically mention Franz Boas because of his influence on W.E.B. Du Bois' thinking and writing about matters of race. Though a century has passed since Du Bois first wrote about the racial dilemma in America, his commentary remains as potent and clairvoyant as ever. For a discussion of the relationship between Franz Boas and W.E.B. Du Bois see Lorini, *Rituals of Race* 76–89. Also see the concise and insightful discussion concerning Du Bois in Robert Michael Franklin, *Liberating Visions: Human Fulfillment and Social Justice in African-American Thought* (Minneapolis: Fortress, 1990) 43–73.

[20] Omi and Winant, "Racial Formations," 19.

[21] Sidney I. Dorbin, "Race and the Public Intellectual: A Conversation with Michael Eric Dyson," in Gary A. Olson and Lynn Worsham, eds., *Race, Rhetoric, and the Postcolonial* (Albany: State University of New York Press, 1999) 105.

[22] We consider ourselves American in that our blood, sweat, and tears had as much, if not more, to do with the building of the nation as those of any other racial group. Despite the similar cultural experiences of African Americans and white Americans, which result from living in the same country, C. Eric Lincoln insisted upon the distinctiveness of African American culture. He wrote, "While Blackamericans [sic] and white Americans share the same value structure informed by the same Judeo-Christian ethic . . . it is the interpretation brought to those common values in day-to-day human intercourse

and the way they are translated into human experience which set one group apart from the other." See Lincoln, *Race, Religion, and the Continuing American Dilemma* (New York: Hill and Wang, 1984) 137.

[23] Peter Paris has demonstrated how, in the face of the loss of tribal identity, the concept of race has served as a form of social cohesiveness for Africans in America. Paris remarks: "Slaveholders identified their African slaves by the category of race, which they described both stereotypically and pejoratively. The slaves also employed the category of race in describing their own collective identity though they imbued it with positive value. . . . Wholly repulsed by racism, African Americans made the term *race* into a prophetic principle of social change. That is to say, whenever they used the term *race, African, Negro, Colored,* they were reconstituting themselves into a new tribal unity in which they sought to preserve their dignity and self-respect, even though the majority population treated them as pariahs." See Paris, *The Spirituality of African Peoples: The Search for a Common Moral Discourse* (Minneapolis: Fortress, 1995) 73.

[24] For examples of how the earliest Christians understood Jesus, and especially his death and resurrection as the "rejected stone" that became the "cornerstone" (i.e., the large stone in ancient architecture upon which much of the foundation rested), see Matt 21:42, Acts 4:11, Eph 2:20, and 1 Pet 2:7.

[25] It was precisely the manner of Jesus' death that constituted, according to Paul in 1 Cor 1:23, "the stumbling block to the Jews and foolishness to the Gentiles." Luke Johnson writes: "Ultimately, it was not the confession of Jesus as Messiah that divided Christians from other Jews. . . . It was the confession of a crucified sinner as resurrected Lord that was divisive." *The Writings of the New Testament: An Interpretation* (rev. ed. Minneapolis: Fortress, 1999) 117.

[26] Kelly Brown Douglas, *Sexuality and the Black Church: A Womanist Perspective* (Maryknoll, N.Y.: Orbis, 1999) 123.

[27] Alice Walker, *In Search of Our Mother's Gardens: Womanist Prose* (New York: Harcourt, Brace, Jovanovich, 1983) xii.

[28] Paris, *The Spirituality of African Peoples* 118.

[29] On the issue of social liberation Cornel West remarks: "Human liberation occurs only when people participate substantively in the decision-making processes in the major institutions which regulate their lives." See West, *Prophesy Deliverance: An Afro-American Revolutionary Christianity* (Philadelphia: Westminster, 1982) 112.

[30] For a probing discussion of African American intellectual life see William M. Banks, *Black Intellectuals: Race and Responsibility in American Life* (New York: W. W. Norton & Company, 1996).

[31] Recent archeological findings have established that the historical Jesus probably had African features (e.g., curly hair, broad nose, thick lips, and dark

skin). For many persons this information may have been a "discovery," but countless black people have argued this fact for generations. The consternation that this "news" has generated among certain white people is quite telling. See Brad R. Braxton, "Guess Who's Coming To Dinner: The Black Jesus and Easter," *Chicago Tribune* (Friday, April 13, 2001).

[32] For recent attempts to seize hermeneutical control of biblical interpretation and theological studies from the vantage point of African-centered scholarship see Randall C. Bailey and Jacquelyn Grant, eds., *The Recovery of Black Presence: An Interdisciplinary Exploration* (Nashville: Abingdon, 1995); also see Vincent Wimbush, ed., *African Americans and the Bible: Sacred Texts and Social Textures* (New York: Continuum, 2000). One of Wimbush's leading questions is: "How might putting African Americans at the center of the study of the Bible affect the study of the Bible?" (ibid. 2). I hope that this book offers at least one kind of answer to Wimbush's helpful and provocative query.

[33] By hermeneutic I simply mean the presuppositions and practices of (biblical) interpretation. In a classic and very subtle discussion of hermeneutics, literary scholar Frank Kermode suggests that Hermes, the Olympian messenger god, is "patron of interpreters." Hermes "is the god of going-between: between the dead and the living, but also between the latent and manifest (god, one might say, of the third ear), and between the text, whether plain or hermetic, and the dying generations of its readers." Thus if one wants to remember what hermeneutics is, one need only recall the activities of Hermes, namely, navigating the space between the sender and the receiver, between the text and the reader. See Kermode, *The Genesis of Secrecy: On the Interpretation of Narrative* (Cambridge, Mass.: Harvard University Press, 1979) 1–2.

[34] Anthony Pinn poses a strident challenge to African American Christian theologians. He writes: "It is my contention that African American religious experience extends beyond the formation and practice of black Christianity. . . . That is to say, historically African Americans have participated in a variety of traditions, such as Yorùbá religious practices (attention to the *orisha* or deities), Voodoo (Vodou), Islam, and humanism. . . . The identity of theology and theologians is too intimately tied to the Christian tradition as opposed to the exploration of life-altering questions that arise within the various formations of African American religiosity." *Varieties of African American Religious Experience* (Minneapolis: Fortress, 1998) 1–2. Also, for an exhaustive discussion of the presence of the conjuring tradition in African American religion see Theophus H. Smith, *Conjuring Culture: Biblical Formations of Black America* (New York: Oxford University Press, 1994).

[35] See C. Eric Lincoln's classic study of Black Muslims, *The Black Muslims in America* (3rd ed. Grand Rapids: Eerdmans, 1994).

[36] Vincent L. Wimbush, "Biblical Historical Study as Liberation: Toward an Afro-Christian Hermeneutic," in Gayraud S. Wilmore, ed., *African American*

Religious Studies: An Interdisciplinary Anthology (Durham, N.C.: Duke University Press, 1989) 142–43.

[37] For descriptions of religious life and practice in African American slave communities see Albert J. Raboteau, *Slave Religion: The "Invisible Institution" in the Antebellum South* (New York: Oxford University Press, 1978) 211–88, and Vincent Harding, "Religion and Resistance among Antebellum Slaves, 1800–1860," in Timothy E. Fulop and Albert J. Raboteau, eds., *African-American Religion: Interpretive Essays in History and Culture* (New York: Routledge, 1997) 107–30.

[38] Genovese, *Roll Jordan Roll* 242. Although throughout the history of African American engagements with the Bible a fundamentalist hermeneutic has not been the primary mode of interpretation, Vincent Wimbush has noted the recent rise of fundamentalist interpretive practices among African Americans. Wimbush remarks: "African Americans were not a significant part of the beginnings of the fundamentalist movement in America. Only in recent decades have significant numbers come to embrace in a self-conscious manner fundamentalist ideology and white fundamentalist communities. This phenomenon seems to reflect a rejection of—or at least a relativizing of the importance of—racialist or culturalist perspectives insofar as they are associated with the African American heritage." Wimbush, "The Bible and African Americans: An Outline of an Interpretive History," in Cain Hope Felder, ed., *Stony the Road We Trod: African American Biblical Interpretation* (Minneapolis: Fortress, 1991) 96.

[39] Ibid. 81–97.

[40] Genovese, *Roll Jordan Roll* 211–12. For further discussion of how African Americans transformed the doctrines of white Protestant Christianity see Mechal Sobel, *Trabelin' On: The Slave Journey to an Afro-Baptist Faith* (Princeton: Princeton University Press, 1979) 99–135 and especially 126–28.

[41] Genovese, *Roll Jordan Roll* 235–36. Discussing how African slaves in America created an alternative reality through religious institutions, Peter Paris observes: "During the last quarter of the eighteenth and first half of the nineteenth century, blacks were able to found independent churches, an activity that constituted the first black independence movement in America. In white churches, not only had blacks perceived a deliberate distortion of the Christian gospel but they feared a loss of their own self-respect should they continue indefinitely in a proscribed form of association with whites." *The Social Teaching of the Black Churches* (Philadelphia: Fortress, 1985) 5–6.

[42] Itumeleng J. Mosala, *Biblical Hermeneutics and Black Theology in South Africa* (Grand Rapids: Eerdmans, 1989) 4.

[43] For an insightful and concise discussion of racism in American Christianity see E. Hammond Oglesby, *O Lord, Move This Mountain: Racism and Christian Ethics* (St. Louis: Chalice Press, 1998) 1–31.

[44] Quoted by G.E.M. De Ste. Croix, *The Class Struggle in the Ancient Greek World: From the Archaic Age to the Arab Conquest* (Ithaca: Cornell University Press, 1981) 417.

[45] Martin Luther King, Jr., *Strength to Love* (Philadelphia: Fortress, 1963) 53.

[46] See Gary A. Olson, "Fish Tales: A Conversation with 'The Contemporary Sophist,'" in *Philosophy, Rhetoric, Literary Criticism: (Inter)views* (Carbondale: Southern Illinois University Press, 1994) 55.

[47] For a probing discussion of how one European-American biblical scholar has been challenged by the presence of non-traditional readings from "the margins" see Daniel Patte, "Acknowledging the Contextual Character of Male, European-American Critical Exegeses: An Androcritical Perspective," in Fernando F. Segovia and Mary Ann Tolbert, eds., *Reading from this Place: Social Location and Biblical Interpretation in the United States* (Minneapolis: Fortress, 1995) 35–55.

[48] Nearly thirty years ago Walter Wink, a European-American exegete, also bemoaned the lack of socially relevant biblical scholarship. Wink wrote: "The outcome of biblical studies in the academy is a trained incapacity to deal with the real problems of actual living persons in their daily lives." *The Bible in Human Transformation: Toward a New Paradigm for Biblical Study* (Philadelphia: Fortress, 1973) 6.

[49] James Baldwin, *The Price of the Ticket* (New York: St. Martin's Press, 1985) xix–xx.

[50] Genovese, *Roll Jordan Roll* 2.

[51] Baldwin, *The Price of the Ticket* xv.

[52] Philip Foner, ed., *W.E.B. Du Bois Speaks, 1890–1919*, vol. 1 (New York: Pathfinder Press, 1970) 79.

[53] W.E.B. Du Bois, *The Souls of Black Folk* (Chicago: A.C. McClurg and Co., 1903; reprint New York: Dover Publications, 1994) 2.

2

A Reading Strategy for Liberation

READER-RESPONSE CRITICISM AND
BLACK AND WOMANIST THEOLOGIES

*W*ith a provisional definition of liberation and a cursory discussion of certain factors shaping African American experience in place, it now seems appropriate to turn our attention to the issue of interpretive methodology. I contend that an African American hermeneutic may fruitfully employ reader-response theory. Of the extant versions of reader-response theories, the version that most closely resembles what I am positing is that of Stanley Fish. But as this discussion develops, and the reader-response theory used in this African American hermeneutic is articulated and refined, it will become clear that my version, though dependent on Fish's, is not identical. For example, as will be seen in my exegesis, I believe that my reading is more text-oriented than Fish's.

I hope that the appropriateness of reader-response theory for an African American hermeneutic will become clear. I will explicitly offer, however, one overarching reason for choosing this approach. As Robert Morgan has suggested, literary interpretive frameworks[1] are often more promising for theological aims and interests than, for example, historical interpretive frameworks.[2] Morgan writes:

> A literary framework, which includes the results of historical and linguistic research, is today more promising for the study of religion and for theology than the historical framework (which includes literary study) that

has dominated New Testament studies in particular since the 1830s. . . . Where the aims of biblical interpretation are religious or theological, it is necessary to consider exactly how historical study is important for this, and to recognize its proper place, which may be a subordinate one.[3]

I readily admit that my discussion of African American hermeneutics and the purposes of this entire book are influenced by and in service of black and womanist theologies.[4] Since "the primary responsibility of theology is to articulate anew the faith of its religious community,"[5] my explicit theological agenda requires a greater connection between past and present than is sometimes provided by historical frameworks.[6]

More pointedly, James Cone has articulated the primary responsibility of theology from the vantage point of black theology. He writes:

> Black theology is a theology of liberation. It seeks to plumb the black condition in the light of God's revelation in Jesus Christ, so that the black community can see that the gospel is commensurate with the achievement of black humanity. Black theology is a theology of "blackness." It is the affirmation of black humanity that emancipates black people from white racism, thus providing authentic freedom for both white and black people. It affirms the humanity of white people in that it says no to the encroachment of white oppression.[7]

Black and womanist theologies are primarily concerned with the analysis of African American experience in the light of divine revelation.[8] To whatever degree African Americans believe that "God's word" may be "found" in the Bible,[9] biblical interpretation must be related to the present struggle of being black in a racist society. For a hermeneutic to be called African American it must provide biblical exposition with ramifications for present social experience. Historical methods often are unwilling to reckon fully with contemporary issues such as racism. This unwillingness limits the contributions that historical approaches can make to the aims of black and womanist theologies.[10] In short, literary-critical approaches[11] often allow greater connections to be made between the biblical past and the contemporary situation. Since a theological and political analysis of the contemporary African American situation is the ultimate task of black and womanist theologies, I employ a literary-critical approach, in this case reader-response theory.

Generally, reader-response theory suggests that meaning does not reside solely in the text, simply waiting to be discovered by means of the right intellectual tools. Meaning, rather, is a product that is created from the encounter between text and reader. Anthony Thiselton writes: "Reader-response theories call attention to the active role of communities of readers in constructing what counts for them as 'what the text means.'"[12]

Describing how he came to see the importance of the reader in the creation of meaning, Stanley Fish observes:

> If meaning is embedded in the text, the reader's responsibilities are limited to the job of getting it out; but if meaning develops, and if it develops in a dynamic relationship with the reader's expectations, projections, conclusions, judgments, and assumptions, these activities (the things the reader *does*) are not merely instrumental, or mechanical, but essential, and the act of description must both begin and end with them.[13]

In reader-response theory the rise of the importance of the reader in the creation of meaning entails the relative decline of the importance of the author as the sole arbiter of what the text really means.[14]

The debate between formalist interpretive methods[15] and reader-response theory strikes at the issue of textuality. Roland Barthes offers a definition that begins to capture the vision of textuality purported by reader-response theory. He writes: "The text is plural: it achieves plurality of meaning, an irreducible plurality."[16] Barthes is right, but a qualification is needed.

The text is plural, but the achievement of plurality of meaning is not so much an accomplishment of the text. Rather, this plurality is the accomplishment of the various reading communities engaging with texts. It is the multitude of experiences among various reading communities that gives to texts their irreducible plurality. A brief discussion of the concept of interpretive communities in reader-response theory will now be useful.

Reader-response theory asserts that even if one reads a text in private (e.g., in a room by oneself), one would not be engaging in a private reading, for all readers are members of interpretive communities. These interpretive communities constitute and shape the reader's horizon of expectation, which is the "mind-set, or system of references, which characterizes the reader's finite viewpoint amidst his or her situatedness in time and history."[17] The values, purposes, and goals that hold forth in a reading community will determine not only what a reader identifies as meaning in literature but even what a reader considers to be literature in the first place. Terry Eagleton notes:

We can drop once and for all the illusion that the category "literature" is "objective," in the sense of being eternally given and immutable. . . . There is no such thing as a literary work of tradition which is valuable *in itself*, regardless of what anyone might have said or come to say about it. "Value" is a transitive term: it means whatever is valued by certain people in specific situations, according to particular criteria and in the light of given purposes.[18]

The formal elements that contribute to meaning do not lie simply in the text but in the community's norms and goals, which have been inscribed in a reader. Moreover, these elements themselves do not exist prior to the act of interpretation. They, too, are the result of interpretation.[19] Whereas some formalist readings regard certain pre-understandings that readers bring to the text as hindrances to the *discovery of meaning*, reader-response theory regards these pre-understandings, which are the products of community membership, as foundational for the *creation of meaning*. The authority to create and adjudicate over meaning rests with the interpretive community. On the importance of interpretive communities Fish remarks: "Indeed, it is interpretive communities, rather than either the text or the reader, that produce meaning and are responsible for the emergence of formal features."[20]

Fish's emphasis on the role of the community in the interpretive process is a meaningful contribution to reader-response theory. Given, however, the religious dimensions[21] that have surrounded both the composition and the reception of the Bible by various communities over the millennia, Christian interpreters who would employ reader-response theory may have a special obligation to clarify their understanding of the Bible's authority in relation to interpretive communities.

Those who are skeptical of Fish's notion of the authority of interpretive communities may contend that placing too much emphasis on the interpretive community effectively undercuts the Bible's authority to shape and correct Christian belief and behavior. Such skeptics may further argue that to supplant the textual authority of Milton's *Paradise Lost*, as Fish does, may provide secular critics with impressive examples of intellectual virtuosity. Yet few people organize their lives existentially around Milton's *Paradise Lost*. Christians, on the other hand, have for centuries believed in some sense that the Bible is the "word of God."

The critics of reader-response criticism compel us to raise some crucial questions. If we move our emphasis too far away from the text itself, are we rendering ourselves unable to be addressed "from beyond" by the voice of God? Put another way, if (too much) authority is be-stowed upon the interpretive community, what happens to the author-ity of the Bible? These are serious issues that call for some attention from the Christian exegete who employs reader-response criticism, and we now turn our attention to a brief engagement with these issues.[22]

THE BIBLE AND AUTHORITY IN READER-RESPONSE CRITICISM

To speak of the authority of the Bible concomitantly plunges one into a conversation about the inspiration of the Bible. Traditionally, Christians have believed that the words of the Bible somehow possess "the breath of God."[23] An account of the Bible's authority presupposes some description, however tentative, of the Bible's inspiration, that is, its connection to God.

My discussion of the Bible's inspiration will have two foci. The first involves God's relationship to the composition of the Bible broadly configured (i.e., how the Bible was written). The second involves the ways God's presence is mediated through the Bible for contemporary communities of faith (i.e., what happens when the Bible is read). In the history of Christian practice and scholarship different groups have accentuated at least one of these foci. The reader-response approach I advocate is obviously more interested in the second element, namely, what happens when the Bible is read. Nonetheless, by reflecting on the role of inspiration in the composition of the Bible I will clarify what I think should (and perhaps often does) happen when contemporary communities read the Bible.

One must assume a crucial characteristic about the nature of God in order to speak intelligibly of God's "involvement" in the writing of the Bible. This assumption, which is the bedrock of the Christian faith, is that God has revealed (and does reveal) aspects of God's nature to hu-manity. In short, just as the discussion of authority presupposes a dis-cussion of inspiration, so too a discussion of inspiration presupposes a discussion of divine revelation.[24]

One formulation of the doctrine of revelation maintains that even though many elements of God's nature are beyond the reach of human analysis and imagination, God, nevertheless, has graciously decided to reveal aspects of God's nature to humanity. God is both subject (i.e., originator) and object (i.e., content) of the revelation. Yet, as Sandra Schneiders adroitly suggests, revelation is only effective if there is someone to receive it.[25] Schneiders observes, "To be accessible to us, to invite us into divine intimacy, God has to approach us . . . in and through perceptible reality."[26]

Thus God's revelation is mediated through human experiences, and human participants in those experiences attempt to testify to the experiences through language. As humans record and interpret these experiences in language, the words themselves are not the divine reality but rather point to the divine reality. Words are records of the revelation. In this sense I affirm that the biblical texts left by the authors and their communities are inspired *in their composition.* Believing that they were participants of revelatory experiences with God, these people sought to testify about those experiences in spoken (and eventually written) language.

Obviously, in ancient Israel and the early Church there were countless persons and communities who claimed to have had experiences with God, which they wanted to express and chronicle. This process produced in Judaism and early Christianity a plethora of religious texts[27]—texts that in one way or another claimed to be inspired by God. At this point one may begin to see the inherent difficulty of simply understanding inspiration as an experience with divine reality that prompts one to testify to that experience. Many persons in Jewish and Christian antiquity claimed to have had such experiences. Therefore unless one possessed a rubric to distinguish "legitimate" from "illegitimate" claims there would be no way to distinguish one text's claim of inspiration from another.

Religious, or more specifically theistic texts are produced when persons attempt to codify their experiences with God in language. This process of codification, however, does not in and of itself catapult these religious texts to the status of "Scripture." Scriptures are religious writings that a *community* deems to be reliable mediators of "an encounter with the transcendent."[28] In spite of the large number of religious texts that both ancient Israel and early Christianity composed, the history of canonization of both the Jewish and Christian Bibles[29] demonstrates that not all "religious writings" in these religious movements were elevated to the status of Scripture.

As Jewish and Christian communities read (or more probably heard)[30] certain texts, they became convinced that their interactions with these texts were profitable for forming and developing communities that bore the character of God. Those texts that were most useful for community formation and religious development were elevated to the status of

Scripture. As Israel and the early Church assembled texts that would guide their formations there was no "self-evident" criterion called "inspiration" by which some religious writings were accepted as authoritative and others rejected as non-authoritative. Rather, the designation "inspiration" was a byproduct of a religious text's *usefulness* in a religious community.[31] In light of this one can affirm that the community of faith preceded the Scriptures.

Second Timothy 3:16, a touchstone passage in the debates about the Bible's inspiration, clearly indicates that certain early Christians considered inspiration to be a function of a religious text's communal value. The Greek of 2 Tim 3:16 can be rendered in one of two ways: "All scripture is inspired by God and profitable for teaching, for reproof, for correction, for training in righteousness," or "Every scripture[32] inspired by God is profitable for teaching, for reproof, for correction, for training in righteousness."

Regardless of how one renders this verse, the key indicator of inspiration is usefulness in the community (i.e., the texts that are Scripture are "profitable[33] for teaching, for reproof, for correction, for training in righteousness."). The assertion that a religious writing is useful is itself an interpretive claim or an estimation brought to bear by the community that is hearing or reading the text. James Barr writes: "Why is it important, according to 2 Timothy, that scripture is inspired? Because of its *practical effects*, in teaching and training."[34] There is a Christian Bible because our foreparents in the faith interpreted certain religious texts as more useful in religious formation than other texts.

Let us summarize our observations thus far. I contend that the Bible is inspired in the sense that it contains testimonies of people's encounters with transcendent reality. Divine revelation led to the composition of texts. Subsequently the communities who read, heard, and interpreted these religious texts deemed them to be useful in religious formation, and they elevated these religious texts to the authoritative status of "Scripture." This important historical process explains how the texts of the Bible may have been inspired for ancient Israel and the early Church, but it does not adequately explain why these texts are still considered to be "inspired" for contemporary communities of faith. For an adequate response to this issue, other factors must enter the discussion.

When contemporary communities of faith assert that the Bible is inspired they are making a historical and theological claim that is rooted in faith. First let us consider the *historical* nature of this faith claim.

   Contemporary communities who appeal to Scripture are affirming their faith in the essential correctness of our religious forebears' decisions concerning which texts most helpfully articulate the contours of the Christian faith.[35] Without necessarily passing judgment on the relevance of the specific contents of the Bible for current practice, contemporary Christian communities believe that the writers of Scripture were giving testimony to the revelation of God and God's Messiah that was useful for the community, even if those testimonies possessed the foibles of human production. Out of respect for the historical proximity of these useful testimonies to the foundational events that they recount, we believe that these texts have provided a basic framework for Christian existence.[36]

   Robin Scroggs offers us the valuable concept of biblical texts as "foundational documents." Scroggs writes: "By foundational documents I mean that they [the biblical texts] are those documents that have elicited, set the basic agenda for, and defined what Christianity means as a *historical* reality. A Christian may disagree with what he or she reads in the texts; a Christian cannot refuse serious dialogue with the texts without calling into question the rights of using the term 'Christian' as a self-designation."[37] Thus when contemporary Christian communities read the Bible they acknowledge a robust respect for and even faith in the historical experiences of our religious forebears as they struggled to give witness to divine revelation.

   When contemporary Christian communities read the Bible they also make a faith claim that is more explicitly *theological.* These communities believe that as they read the Scriptures bequeathed to them by Christian history God *may* speak fresh words of revelation. The Scriptures are not the word of God *per se,* but the Scriptures possess the potential to become the word of God as they are read faithfully and creatively under the auspices of the Holy Spirit[38] and in light of the community's ongoing experiences. Thus we read the Scriptures and invite the Holy Spirit in our midst to help us discern what in the text is supposed to speak to us and how it is supposed to speak.

   My affirmation that the Scriptures are not inherently the word of God may seem shocking to some, and downright blasphemous to others. Yet I would remind readers that there is a long and respected tradition in Judaism and Christianity of understanding the word of God as a reality that is larger than the biblical text itself. For example, in rabbinic Judaism the commandments of God were not and are not identified simply with

the written words of the Torah. The commandments of God also include the oral Torah, or the ongoing interpretations of the written text
in light of new circumstances.[39] Barry Holtz writes: "On Mount Sinai
God gave not only the Written Torah that we know, but the Oral Torah,
the interpretations of the Jews down through time."[40]

Furthermore, the apostle Paul, reflecting his Jewish heritage, suggests
in Rom 10:17 that the word of God is not the text *per se,* but the interpretation of the Christ event. For Paul the interpretation of the Christ
event surely would have involved reflection on the texts of the Jewish
Bible, but the Christ event and any interpretations of it expanded far
beyond the simple words on the page of the text. Paul writes: "So faith
comes from what is heard, and what is heard comes through the word
of Christ." One way of understanding the import of Rom 10:17 is not to
start with the beginning of the verse and read forward, but rather to
start with the end of the verse and read backward.

The word of Christ in this verse is probably Paul's way of referring
to preaching, and preaching for Paul would have involved the oral interpretation of the texts of Judaism read through the lens of Jesus Christ.[41]
Thus Paul believed that when the texts of Judaism were read and proclaimed in the light of the death, resurrection, and imminent return of
Jesus Christ they created a situation of address, or what Paul labels in
Rom 10:17 as "hearing."

The living voice of God that addresses persons is not simply the
words of the biblical text, but the words of the text as they are interpreted for the needs and concerns of the *present* community. When one
responds to the address of God with openness and acceptance, this
creates faith, or perhaps is a description of faith. Faith, in other words,
is not intellectual assent to a "laundry list" of dogmas, but an active
process of disciplined listening for and to the living voice of God's Spirit
that occurs in the process of interpretation. Thus Paul teaches us that
the word of God is not a static quality latent in the words on the page,
but a dynamic process, even event that occurs when communities read
the text through the lens of Christ and in the light of current needs.

With a kind of faithful openness both to the text and, more impor-
tantly, to the Holy Spirit, a community should read the Scriptures. A
community's interpretations may confirm its assumptions and presuppositions about God, about the community itself, and about the world.
On the other hand, its interpretations may overturn those assumptions
and presuppositions, replacing them with new ones. To use Thomas
Long's words, the Scriptures are the "meeting ground,"[42] a reliable place

where the contemporary community gathers, hopeful for and, in fact, expectant of a word from God. Thus the contemporary reading community finally considers the Scriptures inspired not because they chronicle the revelatory experiences of our forebears in the faith, but because these texts, when engaged by the community under the leadership of the Holy Spirit, may emit God's revealing voice for us *in the here and the now.*

Contrary to the protestations of certain critics, reader-response approaches do not simply guarantee that the community will reconfirm its own assumptions.[43] It is not the text that makes claims upon the community. Rather, the Holy Spirit speaks to, through, and sometimes contrary to the experiences of the community as the community reads the text.[44] It is this sometimes messy and always mysterious interaction among the Holy Spirit, the community's experiences, and the Scriptures that creates or mediates the word of God.

Yet we must honestly admit that some Christian communities are notorious for ignoring or trying to suppress the word of God. Notable examples would include certain Christian communities' long-time support of chattel slavery, silence and inactivity during the Holocaust, and even the ongoing oppression of women by certain segments of the Christian church. Yet in every age, and in every community, the Spirit is not left without a witness, and the Spirit will send or raise up prophets in communities.[45] These prophets will see different things in the world and in the Scriptures, and their testimony (hopefully and eventually) will convict and convince communities to see things—in the world, in the biblical text, and in themselves—differently.[46]

In light of this description of a communal engagement with the biblical text, I believe that authority is not so much a property of the biblical text as it is a way of talking about various communal processes with the text. The community believes that the biblical text is an indispensable ingredient in the process of shaping and reshaping the Christian community. Yet the community does not fall prostrate before the text, becoming completely subservient to its claims.

Rather, with an unflinching commitment to dialogue with the biblical text the community goes to the text in study, worship, preaching, and theological scholarship. Sometimes the community will read with the text, and at other times the community will read against the text. Regardless of the manifold ways that the community may engage the text, the community believes that if it talks with the text long enough, the Holy Spirit may speak.

THE AFRICAN AMERICAN (CHRISTIAN)
INTERPRETIVE COMMUNITY

Having introduced the meaning and role of interpretive communities, I shall identify more concretely the primary interpretive community from and of which I speak in this book. Whereas some scholars, when discussing interpretive communities, appear to have academic interpretive communities more in mind, I am more interested in the reading community of African Americans without advanced training in biblical studies. In 1991 there were hardly more than thirty black North Americans with completed Ph.D.s in biblical studies.[47] In 2000, this number had risen slightly to forty-five.[48] Furthermore, a large number of African Americans have never had any advanced academic or professional training in any academic discipline. Thus many African Americans might be classified as "non-professional" readers.

Liberation strategies must be capable of being utilized by those uninitiated in the ways of the academy as well as by those with advanced academic training.[49] Otherwise, the geometric shape of the African American community will be that of a triangle instead of the preferred circle. The goal in a triangle is to have a company of the elect and enlightened elite at the top who descend occasionally from their positions of privilege in order to point the masses toward freedom. In a circle, the goal is radical interdependence. The contributions made by various persons in the African American community and the benefits they receive are lost in an endless cycle of interdependence. My readings of Scripture take seriously the experiences of African American lay persons who might work on construction crews and in cafeterias as well as those who have risen to some prominence, for example, in the world of business. Some further clarification of the identity of my reading community, however, is needed.

When I say that my interpretive community is the African American community I am not denying that I am also a member, at the same time, of other communities. Stanley Fish notes: "Each of us is a member of not one but innumerable interpretive communities in relation to which different kinds of belief are operating with different weight and force."[50] Yet in spite of the innumerable interpretive communities to which I belong, the community whose beliefs exert the strongest and most persistent force upon me (and upon many African Americans) is the larger African American community. Thus when conflicts arise between the values of two interpretive communities to which I belong, the African American community's values have traditionally provided significant criteria for the resolution of the conflict.

Critics may object to the above formulation, contending that my identification of the African American community as my primary interpretive community is imprecise and too generic to have any real force. To be sure, African American experience is multifarious or "imprecise," but, in spite of the myriad manifestations of it, there is a thread running through African American experience that stitches together the sundry patches into a quilt. That thread is the communal quest of African Americans for legitimate self-affirmation.

Again critics may object, noting that a communal quest for self-affirmation is a contradiction because self-affirmation is an individual or psychological quest. But in most cultures one's self-image is related, however loosely, to one's position in a larger group. The interplay between communal and individual identities is certainly present in white culture, but it is much more pronounced in African American culture.[51] Even in dominant white American society, which often promulgates a doctrine of individualism, in order for one to have a healthy self-image one must find some place in relation to the larger society. In African American experience self-image and self-affirmation are not simply related to the society of other African Americans; they are, rather, inextricably tied to that society. Whether the members of our society are successful or not, they are still members of the African American community as long as they preserve this organic link with the community by acknowledging their blackness, which entails a conscious choice to accept the joys and woes of African American history and of our current struggles.[52]

This begins to get at the heart of what I discussed in Chapter One concerning how, in the African American context, "blackness" cuts across divisions (e.g., social class and religious denominations),[53] which can and have been so divisive in other cultural contexts. For instance, the African American community is not monolithic as it relates to socioeconomic class. African Americans can be found at all strata, from the wealthy and well-educated to the poor and illiterate. One might think that these class differences would create considerable barriers to communication among African Americans, and occasionally they do.

Nevertheless, I also believe that certain common themes of African American experience, which I am endeavoring to name, are often stronger and more important than the class differences. These themes enable black folks to communicate and share bonds even when one might think that common ground was impossible to find. Even though I am a middle-class, well-educated man, I have not had difficulty relating to other African Americans from lower economic classes and with fewer educational achievements, because the larger experiences of being African American have provided a platform for conversation irrespective of other differences that may have existed. I offer an illustration.

At the various universities where I have received my formal training, and even at the university where I currently teach, I have shared an almost ineffable bond with the African American men and women who have worked in the cafeterias as servers and as custodians. During my sojourns in these institutions, these men and women have been some of my most insightful teachers. On the many occasions that I have met and talked with these working-class black folks I have sought to listen to them intently. One of my colleagues suggests that when one is in the presence of greatness one should take notes. By the standards of some, these working-class black folks would be considered anything but great because of their relatively lower incomes and educational achievements. I have intuited, however, that their dignity and perseverance in spite of their struggles is precisely what constitutes their greatness. Thus even if I have not taken written notes as they have talked with me, I have taken copious mental notes.

If one were to analyze the various dialogues I have had with these men and women, one would hear the pride in their voices and the gratitude in mine. Their pride has emanated from the fact that my very presence and success at these universities have meant that their struggles (and the struggles of countless African Americans like them across the ages) have not been in vain. The gratitude in my voice has emanated from my knowledge that my presence and success, regardless of my personal abilities, have had much to do with their struggles. I was "taller" than they precisely because I was standing on their shoulders.

I am hesitant to pin down too exactly what constitutes African American experience for reasons already enumerated, but of the many things that comprise African American experience there is this persistent quest for self-affirmation, which means not only an affirmation of the self but also of the African American culture, which gives rise to and nourishes the self.

Another defining feature is a conscious effort to accept our history and the responsibility of our struggles. Eugene Genovese nicely illuminates this point. He writes: "Whereas Western civilization bequeathed to Euro-Americans a vision of being heirs of the ages, African civilization bequeathed to the Afro-American a vision of being debtors to the ages, and accordingly a sense of responsibility to those who came before."[54] Thus when the "mother" of my home church in Virginia[55] said to me lovingly but frankly, "Boy, don't get educated away from your people," she was expressing her pride in me but also reminding me of my responsibility to her and to all my forebears. In this book *I* am speaking. Yet because of what self-affirmation means in African American experience, to say that I am speaking is also to say that, in some meaningful but not totalizing way, the African American community, whose struggles and aspirations have been inscribed in me, is speaking.[56]

Having identified my primary interpretive community, I want to address a particular challenge of constructing an African American hermeneutic. A potential criticism of an African American hermeneutic is the apparent lack of common ground it offers to non-African Americans who wish to discuss the interpretations yielded by this hermeneutic. This criticism arose when I shared my interpretive approach with a person who noted that my hermeneutic reminded him of the famous dialogue between Jesus and Nicodemus in John 3. My interlocutor suggested that in effect I was telling dominant groups that they would not understand what I was saying unless they were "born anew." Furthermore, my interlocutor was concerned to know where, if at all, was the common ground in an African American hermeneutic. His comments drove me to re-examine that famous passage in John 3.

As I understand that passage, Nicodemus's tragic (mis)understanding came because he was holding on to a conceptual framework that was inappropriate in this age when the Kingdom of God was dawning. Nicodemus's conception of being "born anew" caused him to (mis)understand being "born anew" as re-entering the womb. Yet Jesus, when explaining his understanding of being "born anew," appeals, interestingly enough, to the concept of *experience*.

Jesus declares to Nicodemus: "Do not at all be amazed that I said to you, 'You must be born anew.' The wind blows wherever it wills, and you hear its sound, but you do not know whence it comes or whither it goes; so it is with every one who has been born of the Spirit."[57] In other words, the acid test of being "born anew" is not some cognitive apprehension of the concept ("you do not know whence the wind comes or whither it goes"), but the effects of the wind or the experience of it ("you hear its sound").

In this story common ground is available, but Jesus dictates the terms of what constitutes common ground. The misunderstanding could have been overcome, but Nicodemus would have had to relinquish his inappropriate conceptual framework. David Rensberger offers further insight on this point. He writes, "Nicodemus is challenged [by Jesus] to join the action of God in the unfamiliar and the improbable."[58] To enter the kingdom, Nicodemus must be "born anew" in the sense that Jesus means.

I see the dialogue between Jesus and Nicodemus as a provocative metaphor for the state of race relations between blacks and whites in America. For far too long blacks and whites, like Jesus and Nicodemus, have talked past one another because the communities have operated from vastly different conceptual frameworks. Many African Americans have wanted to say to our white colleagues, "If you are *really* interested in contributing to better and more equitable relationships with us, you must be born anew."

When the phrase "you must be born anew" is passed through the filter of African American experience it comes out, "you must become black."[59] "Black" is here understood metaphorically to mean a thoroughgoing and imaginative attempt on the part of whites to view the world from another vantage point than their current position of privilege and power. Such efforts on the part of white persons, especially those who are Christians, are more than exercises in sympathetic understanding. Such efforts begin to usher in the subversion of traditional power dynamics that, I believe, typifies an allegiance to the inbreaking kingdom of God. I believe that many African Americans are curious to know how many whites are willing to demonstrate in "broad daylight" their solidarity with the inbreaking kingdom instead of merely inquiring about it, like Nicodemus, in the shadows of anonymity.

As I argued in Chapter One, there are limits to how completely even the most understanding white persons can enter the black experience. Nevertheless, if white persons are truly interested in establishing common ground with African Americans, white persons must be willing to undergo "conversions" in their cultural conceptual frameworks.

I offer some anecdotal evidence about the need for "cultural conversion" among our white brothers and sisters. My wife once had a conversation with a white colleague at work who happened to be looking at a picture of an antebellum plantation home. My wife's colleague remarked, "Could you imagine living in one of these [plantation homes]?" In response, my wife suggested that she could not imagine *living* in a plantation, but she could imagine what it must have been like to *work* on a plantation (as a slave). In short, my wife's white colleague, even when talking to an African American, lacked the cultural sensitivity to realize that the wealth to build such plantations and the leisure to enjoy them were the direct result of white domination of African Americans.

Another example may be instructive. In a large academic seminar I once heard a colleague refer to "continental philosophy," which, of course, for that colleague (and presumably for everyone else) was supposed to mean *European* philosophy. I did not want to disrupt the seminar presentation, and so I remained silent. Yet the following thoughts raced through my mind:

> Which *continent* do you mean? Can we be so presumptuous as to think that *the continent* should invoke Europe in people's minds? As far as I am concerned, any reference to *the continent* must really be a reference to Africa, since scientists agree that human life emerged from sub-Saharan Africa and that all persons have some traces of ancient African genes in them.

I am fully persuaded that the comments of my wife's colleague and my colleague were not meant to convey any malice or prejudice. The comments were made without even thinking about the cultural assumptions they communicated, which is precisely the point. White privilege is so inscribed in our culture that it is perpetuated without anyone even thinking about it. Conversion is necessary if common ground is to be established.

Such conversions will include, but not be limited to, honest admissions of how thoroughly the political, cultural, and economic scales have been (and continue to be) tipped in favor of white culture. Conversions will also entail active involvement in processes, be they individual, familial, local, or national, which contribute to the dismantling of the structures of unjustified cultural privilege. In short, as in the case of Nicodemus, being "born anew" comes with a "price tag" attached.

By boldly presenting another vantage point from which to perceive the world and the biblical text an African American hermeneutic challenges white culture and white biblical scholarship to confess that its approaches to knowledge, language, and (the Christian) religion are not, after all, absolute but instead culturally-conditioned fragments of truth. When a (dominant) community realizes that at best it holds only fragments of truth it should begin to seek genuine conversation with other (non-dominant) communities who also possess fragments of truth. The more that fragments of truth mix, mingle, collide, but above all converse with one another, the more likely it is that liberation will occur for all parties involved. In short, there can be no common ground as long as white culture assumes that it is the sole owner of the field. An African American hermeneutic is a sobering reminder that there are other persons who can rightly claim joint ownership.

NOTES: CHAPTER 2

[1] Traditionally, literary frameworks have been more interested in exploring the experiences of (ancient and modern) *readers*.

[2] Traditionally, historical frameworks have been more interested in ascertaining the "intentions" and "aims" of the *authors* of (ancient) texts.

[3] Robert Morgan, with John Barton, *Biblical Interpretation* (Oxford: Oxford University Press, 1988) 286–87.

[4] According to George Cummings, "From its inception, then, black theology had as its central concern the identification of racism and racist values within theology and the church, as well as the establishment of a new paradigm for the evolution of black theological discourse." Furthermore, black theology seeks to "evolve an explicit analysis of the religio-cultural traditions, values, and symbols that define African-American life." See Cummings, "New Voices in Black Theology: The African-American Story as a Source of Emancipatory Rhetoric," in James H. Cone and Gayraud S. Wilmore, eds., *Black Theology: A Documentary History* (Maryknoll, N.Y.: Orbis, 1993) 2:71–72. For classic discussions of black theology see James H. Cone, *Black Theology and Black Power* (enlarged ed. San Francisco: HarperSan Francisco, 1989), and J. Deotis Roberts, *Liberation and Reconciliation: A Black Theology* (Philadelphia: Westminster, 1971). Delores Williams defines womanist theology as the attempt "to help black women see, affirm, and have confidence in the importance of their experience and faith for determining the character of the Christian religion in the African-American community. Womanist theology challenges all oppressive forces impeding black women's struggle for survival and for the development of a positive, productive quality of life conducive to women's and family's freedom and well-being." *Sisters in the Wilderness: The Challenge of Womanist God-Talk* (Maryknoll, N.Y.: Orbis, 1993) xiv. The recent anthology *Embracing the Spirit: Womanist Perspectives on Hope, Salvation, and Transformation,* edited by Emilie M. Townes (Maryknoll, N.Y.: Orbis, 1997) has demonstrated how expansive womanist theological reflection has become. In earlier moments in the histories of black and womanist theologies there may have been some sub-

stantive differences between these two theological approaches. For the development of womanist theology as a related but distinct outgrowth of black theology see Kelly Brown Douglas, "Womanist Theology: What Is Its Relationship to Black Theology?" in *Black Theology: A Documentary History* 2:290–99. Yet in spite of the differences of approach that may still exist, black and womanist theologies seek to create a critical dialogue between indigenous African American experiences and serious God-talk. Moreover, both of these theologies attempt to establish healthy dialogue between African American women and men.

[5] Morgan, *Biblical Interpretation* 283.

[6] Schubert Ogden contends that we reflect on "what has been thought, said, and done in the past" in order to shed light on its meaning for the present. Unfortunately, in traditional biblical scholarship many interpreters have not shared Ogden's perspective. Thus they have often summarily dismissed questions of present meaning. See Ogden, *Doing Theology Today* (Valley Forge, Pa.: Trinity Press International, 1996) 33.

[7] James H. Cone, "Black Theology as Liberation," in Gayraud S. Wilmore, ed., *African American Religious Studies: An Interdisciplinary Anthology* (Durham, N.C.: Duke University Press, 1989) 177.

[8] By "divine revelation" I mean the contents and forms by which the nature of God is revealed.

[9] Itumeleng Mosala underscores the need to realize the "ideological" nature of calling the Bible the "Word of God." Mosala notes: "The notion that the Bible is simply the revealed 'Word of God' is an example of an exegetical framework that is rooted in such an idealist epistemology. I criticize that position . . . because it leads to a false notion of the Bible as nonideological, which can cause political paralysis in the oppressed people who read it." *Biblical Hermeneutics and Black Theology in South Africa* (Grand Rapids: Eerdmans, 1989) 5–6. Below I will briefly discuss my understanding of biblical authority.

[10] Nevertheless, reader-response criticism is not averse to employing other methodologies when producing its interpretations. Edgar McKnight observes: "Reader-response approaches are capable of accommodating and utilizing approaches followed in more conventional biblical and literary studies. Historical and sociological exegeses, for example, are not precluded in reader-response criticism. They are reconceptualized and relativized but not made illegitimate as such." See McKnight, "Reader-Response Criticism," in Steven L. McKenzie and Stephen R. Haynes, eds., *To Each Its Own Meaning: Biblical Criticisms and Their Application* (Louisville: Westminster John Knox, 1999) 240. The interpretations that I will offer employ insights from historical criticism when appropriate. Yet by using the African American experience as the ultimate critical principle, these readings will, I hope, represent a move from dependence on dominant interpretations.

[11] Literary approaches to New Testament interpretation are time-honored, traditional methods. For example, form criticism, in its heyday, was commonly referred to as literary criticism. In form criticism, the exegete analyzes a unit of the biblical text called a "pericope" and classifies it according to its form (e.g., a miracle story or a controversy story). Once the form is properly identified, the exegete attempts to reconstruct the historical situation in the life of Israel, Jesus, or the early Church that could have spawned such a unit of literature. In short, form criticism is ultimately a method to reconstruct the history of a text's author and first recipients. More contemporary modes of literary criticism espouse the position that biblical texts are not simply windows to the history behind texts. Texts also aim to create a world for contemporary readers to enter, and the meanings of a text emerge (or are created) as the readers move in the world of a text. J. Severino Croatto suggests that the truly important aspect of interpretation is not what is behind the text but what is ahead of the text, or "what it suggests as a pertinent message for the life of the one who receives it or seeks it out." See Croatto, *Biblical Hermeneutics: Toward a Theory of Reading as the Production of Meaning* (Maryknoll, N.Y.: Orbis, 1987) 50.

[12] Anthony C. Thiselton, *New Horizons in Hermeneutics: The Theory and Practice of Transforming Biblical Reading* (Grand Rapids: Zondervan, 1992) 515.

[13] Stanley Fish, *Is There a Text in This Class?: The Authority of Interpretive Communities* (Cambridge, Mass.: Harvard University Press, 1980) 2–3.

[14] In his classic work on hermeneutical theory, Hans-Georg Gadamer provocatively explored the relationship among text, reader, and meaning. He wrote: "To understand it [literature] does not mean primarily to reason one's way back into the past, but to have a present involvement in what is said. It is not really about a relationship between persons, between the reader and the author (who is perhaps quite unknown), but about sharing in the communication that the text gives us. This meaning of what is said is, when we understand it, quite independent of whether we can gain from the tradition a picture of the author and of whether or not the historical interpretation of the tradition as a literary source is our concern." See Gadamer, *Truth and Method* (London: Sheed & Ward, 1975) 353.

[15] Formalism posits that texts are self-sufficient and emit clear, prescribed meanings that can be understood with no reference to the world outside them. For a broad discussion of certain characteristics of formalism see Stanley Fish, *Doing What Comes Naturally: Change, Rhetoric, and the Practice of Theory in Literary and Legal Studies* (Durham, N.C.: Duke University Press, 1989) 5–6.

[16] Roland Barthes, "From Work to Text," in Josué V. Harari, ed., *Textual Strategies: Perspectives in Post-Structural Criticism* (Ithaca: Cornell University Press, 1979) 76.

[17] Thiselton, *New Horizons in Hermeneutics* 34.

[18] Terry Eagleton, *Literary Theory: An Introduction* (Minneapolis: University of Minnesota Press, 1983) 10–11.

[19] In the case of the Bible there are obviously "formal" elements in the text in the sense of signs on the page, or words, that point to other realities. Yet one may contend that these words do not have "meanings" in and of themselves. Certainly it is possible for the modern interpreter, who is equipped with the relevant religious and socio-historical information concerning the biblical world, to ascertain the broad communicative aims or intentions of the authors of biblical texts. Yet for other persons the reconstruction of what biblical authors said or intended to say does not necessarily count for "meaning." Historical reconstruction might be identified as finding the text's meaning if one belongs to a community that understands meaning as the general identification of the historical author's aims. In order to find this kind of meaning, however, one must make various interpretive assumptions (you might even call them "faith claims") that enable the process to proceed. For example, one must assume that the authors of biblical texts were both aware of their intentions and able to present them relatively clearly in language. This assumption seems fairly innocent until one takes into account the psychological "reality" that occasionally we use words not to reveal our intentions but to mask them. Sometimes the unspoken (or unwritten) comes closer to our true intentions than the spoken (or written). Thus an interpretive assumption concerning language's ability to accurately portray an author's intentions must be in place even before one can begin reconstructing those intentions. Yet the identification of some of the intentions of the historical author is not the only meaning of the word "meaning." In another interpretive community persons may construe the "meaning" of a biblical text as its ability to provide spiritual guidance that takes into account the cultural locations of the contemporary readers. The belief that the Bible—a compilation of texts written thousands of years ago by African-Asiatic peoples—has enduring significance *for us* is an interpretation, even a faith claim. When one reads a text as Scripture one assumes that the contemporary context of reading is as important as, if not more important than the historical context of the text's composition. Thus to say that interpretive communities create meaning is not to deny the linguistic "factualness" of the Bible. Rather, it is the honest admission that certain acts of interpretation have already taken place long before we read the first word of any text. For further discussion of the question of what counts for "meaning" in biblical interpretation see Stephen Fowl, "The Ethics of Interpretation or What's Left Over After the Elimination of Meaning," *Society of Biblical Literature Seminar Papers* (Atlanta: Scholars, 1988) 69–81.

[20] Fish, *Is There A Text in This Class?* 14.

[21] Vernon Robbins calls this the "sacred texture" of biblical texts, that is, "their insights into the nature of the relation between human life and the divine."

See Robbins, *Exploring the Texture of Texts: A Guide to Socio-Rhetorical Interpretation* (Valley Forge, Pa.: Trinity Press International, 1996) 120. Also see Luke Johnson's helpful discussion of religious experience in *Religious Experience in Earliest Christianity* (Minneapolis: Fortress, 1998) 60–67.

[22] I enter the forthcoming discussion with fear and trembling, realizing that debates concerning biblical authority can quickly become complex and obscure. Some treatment of these issues is unavoidable if one wants to be theologically responsible and intellectually honest. Yet I am also aware that the goal of the current volume is not to offer theories about biblical interpretation but to provide a biblical interpretation. Steven Kraftchick has cautioned biblical interpreters about spending too much time and energy in methodological queries. See Kraftchick, "Facing Janus: Reviewing the Biblical Theology Movement," in Steven M. Kraftchick, Charles D. Myers, Jr., and Ben C. Ollenburger, eds., *Biblical Theology: Problems and Perspectives* (Nashville: Abingdon, 1995) 77.

[23] James Barr writes: "Inspiration is a rather abstract term: the simpler and more direct term which lies behind it is 'to breathe.'" Thus to say that the Bible is inspired is to say that it contains the "breath of God." See Barr, *Escaping from Fundamentalism* (London: S.C.M. Press, 1984) 1.

[24] See Paul J. Achtemeier, *Inspiration and Authority: Nature and Function of Christian Scripture* (Peabody, Mass.: Hendrickson, 1999) 8.

[25] This observation advanced by Schneiders was also made earlier by Paul Tillich, the noted twentieth-century German theologian. For a discussion of Tillich's use of Scripture see David H. Kelsey, *The Uses of Scripture in Recent Theology* (Philadelphia: Fortress, 1975) 65.

[26] Sandra M. Schneiders, *The Revelatory Text: Interpreting the New Testament as Sacred Scripture* (San Francisco: HarperSan Francisco, 1991) 37. In formulating my understanding of the interaction of the community and the Bible in interpretation I have found Schneiders' book to be a useful dialogue partner. She offers a comprehensive and plausible account of the complex processes that occur in biblical interpretation.

[27] Judaism, especially from the Second Temple period onward (i.e., after the cataclysmic destruction of Solomon's temple in 587 B.C.E. by the Babylonians), and early Christianity were enormously prolific religious movements. For a collection of some of the religious texts produced by Jews and Christians that were not canonized into the Jewish or Christian Bibles see James H. Charlesworth, ed., *The Old Testament Pseudepigrapha*. 2 vols. (New York: Doubleday, 1983), and Wilhelm Schneemelcher, ed., *The New Testament Apocrypha*. 2 vols. (Philadelphia: Westminster, 1964).

[28] John P. Burgess, *Why Scripture Matters: Reading the Bible in a Time of Church Conflict* (Louisville: Westminster John Knox, 1998) 27.

[29] For helpful discussions of the canonization of the Bible see Harry Y. Gamble, *The New Testament Canon: Its Making and Meaning* (Philadelphia: Fortress, 1985) and Lee Martin McDonald, *The Formation of the Christian Biblical Canon* (Nashville: Abingdon, 1988).

[30] Harry Gamble has shown that a majority of early Christians would have been unable to read and write. Yet early Christian gatherings and worship services involved lengthy public readings of authoritative religious literature. Gamble maintains that "Christians who could not read nevertheless became conversant with the substance of scriptural literature and also with other texts that were occasionally read in the setting of worship. Thus, although the limited extent of individual literacy certainly had a bearing on the composition, transcription, private use, and authoritative interpretation of Christian texts, it had little adverse effect on the ability of Christians generally to gain a close acquaintance with Christian literature." *Books and Readers in the Early Church: A History of Early Christian Texts* (New Haven: Yale University Press, 1995) 8–9. Interestingly, a similar process occurred with African American slaves. Many of them were unable to read and write English, yet they acquired significant familiarity with Christian Scripture through the oral tradition. See the discussion of African American experience in Chapter One.

[31] Sandra Schneiders observes: "It is important to note that the Church never considered inspiration the grounds or the criterion for including a writing in the canon, but once a book was canonized, it was regarded as inspired." *The Revelatory Text* 47.

[32] When this passage speaks about the inspiration of Scripture it is, of course, referring to the Scripture of Judaism and not the Christian Bible. When 2 Timothy was written there was no such thing as the New Testament or the Christian Bible. The Bible of Judaism was the Bible for the earliest followers of Jesus.

[33] The Greek word (ὠφέλιμος) that is translated as "profitable" in the New Revised Standard Version also means "useful" or "valuable."

[34] Barr, *Escaping from Fundamentalism* 3 (emphasis added).

[35] Luke Timothy Johnson, *The Writings of the New Testament* (rev. ed. Minneapolis: Fortress, 1999) 608.

[36] For a concise discussion of foundational or original revelatory events see Kelsey, *The Uses of Scripture* 65.

[37] Robin Scroggs, "The Bible as Foundational Document," *Interpretation* 49 (January 1995) 23.

[38] In many ways the reader-response approach I advocate can be firmly situated in the intellectual tradition of postmodernism. Although definitions and theories of postmodernism abound, one of the simplest characteristics of this intellectual movement is its challenge to so-called universal constructs and

"objective" knowledge. Postmodernism claims that all knowledge is local and contextual; that is, knowledge emanates from certain cultural locations and is useful in certain cultural locations. Commenting on the rise of postmodernism in contemporary life, Walter Brueggemann suggests: "Localism means that it is impossible to voice large truth. All one can do is voice local truth and propose that it pertains elsewhere. . . . [As Christians] we voice a claim that rings true in our context, that applies authoritatively to our lived life. But it is a claim that is made in a pluralism where it has no formal privilege." *Texts Under Negotiation: The Bible and Postmodern Imagination* (Minneapolis: Fortress, 1993) 9. Contrary to the claim of Kevin Vanhoozer (*Is There a Meaning in This Text?* [Grand Rapids: Zondervan, 1998] 163), postmodernism is not the denial of transcendence but rather a sobering realization that belief in transcendence is a faith claim. Thus as a postmodern Christian I believe wholeheartedly in the important, ongoing work of the Holy Spirit in biblical interpretation, but I realize that there is no indisputable evidence to which I can appeal that renders this belief immune from challenge.

[39] James L. Kugel and Rowan A. Greer, *Early Biblical Interpretation* (Philadelphia: Westminster, 1986) 64.

[40] Barry W. Holtz, "Midrash," in *Back to the Sources: Reading the Classic Jewish Texts* (New York: Summit Books, 1984) 185. For a concise discussion of the transforming power of oral scriptures (i.e., the process of reading, hearing, interpreting, and preaching the Scriptures), see H. J. Bernard Combrink, "The Rhetoric of Sacred Scripture," in Stanley E. Porter and Thomas H. Olbricht, eds., *Rhetoric, Scripture and Theology* (Sheffield: Sheffield Academic Press, 1996) 107–12.

[41] For a classic discussion of Paul's interpretation of Scripture see Richard B. Hays, *Echoes of Scripture in the Letters of Paul* (New Haven: Yale University Press, 1989) 154–92.

[42] Thomas G. Long, *The Witness of Preaching* (Louisville: Westminster John Knox, 1989) 50.

[43] Vanhoozer, *Is There a Meaning in This Text?* 165–74.

[44] Karl Barth, the noted twentieth-century Swiss theologian, gave classic expression to the importance of the Holy Spirit for the correct interpretation of the Bible. For a discussion of Barth's hermeneutic see Scott C. Saye, "The Wild and Crooked Tree: Barth, Fish, and Interpretive Communities," *Modern Theology* 12 (1996) 435–58.

[45] For a classic and moving exploration of the "prophetic consciousness" see Abraham J. Heschel, *The Prophets* (New York: HarperCollins, 1962). Also, for discussions of the particular ways that black women have raised their prophetic voices in the name of justice see Marcia Y. Riggs, ed., *Can I Get a Witness? Prophetic Religious Voices of African American Women* (Maryknoll, N.Y.: Orbis, 1997).

[46] Stanley Hauerwas remarks: "God certainly uses Scripture to call the Church to faithfulness, but such a call always comes in the form of some in the Church reminding others in the Church how to live as Christians—no 'text' can be substituted for the people of God." See Hauerwas, *Unleashing the Scripture: Freeing the Bible from Captivity to America* (Nashville: Abingdon, 1993) 28.

[47] Cain Hope Felder, ed., *Stony the Road We Trod: African American Biblical Interpretation* (Minneapolis: Fortress, 1991) 1.

[48] See Randall C. Bailey, "Academic Biblical Interpretation among African Americans in the United States," in Vincent L. Wimbush, ed., *African Americans and the Bible* (New York: Continuum, 2000) 707. Although black biblical scholars are celebrating this increase, we are still very aware of the woeful underrepresentation of people of color in general, and of black people in particular, in the guild of professional biblical studies.

[49] Describing some of the characteristics of liberation theology, Christopher Rowland notes that liberation theology "is explored not just in the tutorial or seminar but engages the whole person in the midst of a life of struggle and deprivation. It is a theology which, above all, often starts from the insights of those men and women who have found themselves caught up in the midst of that struggle, rather than being evolved and handed down to them by ecclesiastical or theological experts." "Introduction: The Theology of Liberation," *The Cambridge Companion to Liberation Theology* (Cambridge: Cambridge University Press, 1999) 2. For further discussion of the role of "non-technical" readers in biblical interpretation see Tim Long, "A Real Reader Reading Revelation," *Semeia* 73 (1996) 79–107.

[50] Fish, *Doing What Comes Naturally* 30.

[51] On the inextricable link between communal and individual identities in African American culture, see Peter J. Paris, *The Spirituality of African Peoples: The Search for a Common Moral Discourse* (Minneapolis: Fortress, 1995) 117–27.

[52] Many African Americans are scornful of other African Americans who promote their individual identities by means of severing their connections to African American culture. Noted African American psychologist Na'im Akbar would diagnose African Americans who must "legitimize" themselves by renouncing their connections to black culture as having severe cases of "plantation psychosis." He remarks: "It is important to understand that when African people are in opposition to themselves they are mentally ill. That's what mental illness is. When you work against your own survival, you are 'crazy.' I don't care if you do have a three-piece suit and are a part of the White House Staff. You are crazy. We need black psychology so we can define *for us* what it means to be crazy." *Visions for Black Men* (Tallahassee: Mind Productions and Associates, 1991) 31 (emphasis added).

[53] One cannot deny that denominational heritage has certainly played an important role in African American religious life. Yet my ministerial experiences, both in the local church and the university, suggest that white people have placed much more stock in denominational differences than black people have. Of course I am generalizing to some degree, but I would contend that the first question that many white people may ask of a Christian minister is, "to what denomination does she or he belong?" On the other hand, the first question that many black people may ask of a Christian minister is, "can she or he preach?" Regardless of various doctrinal differences that black Christian groups may have, certain religious and cultural features seem to hold forth across many of the denominational traditions and appear to be more important than those denominational differences.

[54] Eugene D. Genovese, *Roll Jordan Roll: The World the Slaves Made* (New York: Vintage Books, 1974) 213.

[55] In some African American churches the oldest woman in the congregation receives the honorific title "mother of the church." In fact, certain African American churches will have a "Mothers' Board," which is an auxiliary of elderly and respected women who provide examples of godly living and wield incredible influence and authority in congregational life and politics.

[56] By no means am I denying the importance of individual expression and personal preference in African American culture. When African Americans have "insider" conversations among ourselves, we often remark (jokingly, yet seriously) that many white people feel that if they have seen one of us (i.e., an African American), they have seen *all* of us. African Americans are too complex and diverse for one person to speak for all of us. Yet I am suggesting that many African American families and communities deeply (and perhaps indelibly) ingrain certain social attitudes and social skills into their members as mechanisms of communication and survival in a world dominated by white people. To use a term from Greco-Roman history, there is a black *paideia*, which broadly speaking would be the many things that an African American would need to know to be relatively "successful" in our culture and in the broader world. Thus even when one engages in individual expression it is often accomplished in the context of those communal values and skills that are so important in African American communities. For an example of how the inculcation of a black *paideia* supports rather than obliterates individual expression, one may investigate African American Christian preaching. There are numerous African American preachers who have perfected their own peculiar and powerful styles of proclaiming the gospel. Yet these preachers' efforts to hone their religious rhetoric have been sponsored by the larger appreciation in black culture for rhetorical virtuosity. Since so many other means of personal and institutional achievement have been barred to African Americans, we have always viewed rhetorical aptitude as a means of self- and communal expression. Since

black culture values (religious) rhetoric so highly, individual black preachers have worked hard to be accomplished in their preaching. Yet the individual accomplishments of so many black preachers have only increased the value of rhetoric in African American culture. The communal value sponsors individual expression. The individual expression underscores the communal value. As Henry Louis Gates has intimated, black rhetoric, whether secular or religious, is a way that black people communicate with one another and navigate the wide chasm between black and white cultures. *The Signifying Monkey: A Theory of Afro-American Literary Criticism* (New York: Oxford University Press, 1988).

[57] This is my translation of John 3:7-8.

[58] David Rensberger, *Johannine Faith and Liberating Community* (Philadelphia: Westminster, 1988) 114.

[59] This is Frederick Herzog's interpretation of the Johannine notion of being born from above or being born anew. Frederick Herzog, *Liberation Theology: Liberation in the Light of the Fourth Gospel* (New York: Seabury, 1972) 61–67, quoted in Rensberger, *Johannine Faith and Liberating Community* 114.

3

Galatians and
African American Experience

INTRODUCTION

*I*n this chapter I will interpret various sections[1] of Galatians in the light of African American experience. Although my express purpose is to read this ancient text for contemporary insights, my interpretations are, nonetheless, in conversation with the historical realities that would have occasioned Paul's letter to the Galatians. Thus a brief historical overview of this letter is appropriate.

HISTORICAL OVERVIEW

The attempt to situate Galatians in the Pauline chronology is riddled with numerous difficulties. The letter itself offers some internal chronological clues, and the interpreter can glean additional chronological data from the Acts of the Apostles. Let us attend to a few of the historical references in Galatians and bring them into conversation with some of the data in Acts.

In the so-called "autobiographical section" of Galatians (Galatians 1–2) Paul declares that after his call[2] he traveled to Arabia and Damascus (Gal 1:17). Paul adamantly denies that he journeyed to Jerusalem to visit with the apostles as an immediate consequence of his call. Only after a three-year period did he finally visit Jerusalem. During this visit that lasted only fifteen days Paul saw Peter and James the brother of the Lord (Gal 1:18-19).

54

In Gal 2:1 Paul remarks that after fourteen years he made his second visit to Jerusalem. This reference, "after fourteen years" (διὰ δεκατεσ-σάρων ἐτῶν), contains some chronological ambiguity. It is not clear whether Paul is counting these years concurrently or consecutively. A brief explanation is in order.

If Paul is reckoning time concurrently, the fourteen years of which he speaks in 2:1 include the three years he spent in Arabia and Damascus. Thus the events described in 2:1-10 would have occurred eleven years after the three-year-stint in Arabia and Damascus. If Paul is counting consecutively, however, the fourteen years mentioned in 2:1 are in addition to the three years in Arabia and Damascus. Accordingly, the events he describes in 2:1-10 occurred fourteen years after the stay in Arabia and Damascus and thus seventeen years after he experienced his call. Loveday Alexander correctly suggests that the consecutive reading seems more natural.[3] For the sake of clarity I will offer a historical synopsis that assumes that Paul is counting these years consecutively.

Some major scholars date Paul's call to 34 C.E.[4] Assuming this date, from 34 to 37 C.E. Paul would have spent time in Arabia and Damascus (Gal 1:17). Then, according to Gal 1:18, after these three years he made his first trip to Jerusalem. This would place that trip in 37 C.E.

In Gal 2:1 Paul insists that fourteen years after his first visit to Jerusalem he returned for a second visit. Simple calculations would place Paul's second visit to Jerusalem in 51 C.E. With the notable exception that Acts 11:27-30 narrates Paul making an extra visit to Jerusalem, the events in Galatians 1–2 correspond fairly closely to Acts.

Although Acts may cloud the historical picture with respect to Paul's visits to Jerusalem, this writing may, nevertheless, provide plausible information concerning Paul's activities during the fourteen-year period between his first and second visits to Jerusalem. In Gal 1:21 Paul indicates that after his first visit to Jerusalem he "came into the regions of Syria and Cilicia." Without much difficulty one can correlate Paul's words in Gal 1:21 with Luke's report of Paul's first missionary journey in Acts 13–14.

According to Acts, Antioch of Syria served as a missionary launching pad for Paul and Barnabas. During this first missionary journey Paul evangelized persons in Pisidian Antioch, Iconium, Lystra, and Derbe, and these cities were considered the southern part of the Galatian province. Although we are bereft of indisputable historical proof, it is possible that Paul's primary encounter with the Galatians occurred during this missionary trip detailed in Acts 13–14. Possessing some possible insight about Paul's activity during this fourteen-year span, we now turn our attention to the second Jerusalem visit.

In Galatians 2, Paul says the second Jerusalem visit occurred fourteen years after his initial meeting with Peter and James. Many scholars contend that this meeting corresponds with Luke's depiction of the "Jerusalem Conference" in Acts 15, in spite of some differences in detail between the two accounts. According to Galatians 2, at this meeting Paul defends his missionary tactic of not requiring Gentile converts to be circumcised. The Jerusalem leaders gave tacit consent to this practice when they did not compel Titus, a Gentile, to be circumcised. Furthermore, at this meeting these early Christian leaders agreed to a division of missionary labor, with Paul taking the gospel to the Gentiles and James, Cephas, and John ministering to the Jews.

In Gal 2:11-14 Paul rehearses the details of an incident in Antioch involving Cephas, representatives from James, and the Gentile converts in Antioch. Although the conference in Jerusalem had ostensibly resolved the issue of circumcision, the confusion in Antioch concerning table fellowship between Jewish and Gentile Christians reveals that many important issues had not been fully addressed.

Acts mentions at least two other occasions when Paul traveled to or through the Galatian province. Acts 15:36–18:22 recounts Paul's second missionary journey.[5] During the "outbound" leg of this journey Paul again visited churches in Galatia, in towns such as Derbe and Lystra. During this trip Paul founded churches at Philippi, Thessalonica, Corinth, and Ephesus. Furthermore, during his third missionary journey (Acts 18:23–21:14) Paul made another foray into the Galatian province.

Attempts at historical reconstruction reveal that there may have been ample opportunities during his missionary travels for Paul to establish Christian congregations in the Galatian province and to correspond with them. Yet one cannot be sure precisely when Paul penned Galatians. What is sure is that from Paul's vantage point the Galatian churches were on the verge of forfeiting their newfound freedom and returning to the horrors of slavery. African Americans may learn valuable (contemporary) lessons from Paul's (ancient) struggle to prohibit the Galatians' re-enslavement.

INTERPRETATIONS

Traditional interpretations of Galatians have divided the letter into three sections: *history* (Galatians 1–2), *theology* (Galatians 3–4), and *ethics*

(Galatians 5–6). In the main the letter does appear to divide rather neatly into these categories, but they should not be considered mutually exclusive, for there are times when they overlap.[6] One should not treat each section separately, but as constituent parts of Paul's overall defense of his gospel of freedom. In the ensuing interpretations I shall examine representative passages from each section of the letter.

Using African American experience as my primary interpretive guide, I contend that Paul offers to the Gentile Galatian converts (and to other groups that have been marginalized)[7] the criterion of experience as the basis of acceptance by God. In the case of the Galatians it is the experience of faith that was confirmed by the activity of the Holy Spirit. In fact, Paul may value the role of experience highly because it was an experience that transformed him into the apostle to the Gentiles.

As the champion of the importance of experience in the lives of marginalized people, Paul in Galatians provides helpful insights for African Americans. Yet occasionally a small but detectable vestige of Paul's former ideological commitments leads him to positions that may be problematic and potentially dangerous to the African American liberation movement. In short, to a group of people who have suffered agitation and systematic exclusion at the hands of entrenched dominant groups, Paul, in the main, offers golden words of advice and sterling examples of praxis. On the other hand Paul, the ancient freedom fighter, is at times shackled by his ethnic and ideological connection to the group that is the source of the oppression. Paul the would-be liberator, perhaps stands in need of liberation, but that remains to be seen.

A. *Galatians 1:1-9*[8]

1. Paul—an apostle, not from humans, nor through a human, but through Jesus Christ and God the father, who has raised him from the dead—

2. And all the brothers and sisters[9] with me, to the churches of Galatia.

3. Grace to you and peace from God our father and the Lord Jesus Christ,

4. Who gave himself on behalf of our sins in order that he might rescue us from this present evil age according to the will of God our father.

5. To whom be glory for ever and ever. Amen.

6. I am astonished at how quickly you are defecting from the one who called you in the grace of Christ for another gospel.

7. Not that there is another gospel, but there are certain ones who are confusing you and desiring to pervert the gospel of Christ.

8. But even if we, or a messenger from heaven, should preach the gospel to you other than what was preached to you, let him be accursed.

9. As we have said beforehand, and now I say again, if anyone preaches to you a gospel other than what you received, let him be accursed.

From his opening words Paul clearly enunciates that the concept of experience,[10] and not traditional historical norms and standards, is to be the guiding principle of this letter. In 1:1 Paul writes: "Paul, an apostle, not from humans, nor through a human, but through Jesus Christ and God the father who raised him from the dead." Without delay Paul wants his listeners to know that his authority and function have a divine origin.

As an envoy of Christ, an apostle possesses special authority, but the authority is not a consequence of natural ability or talents. Rather, the authority is a derivative of being a specially selected agent of Christ who is charged with proclaiming the gospel. As an apostle, Paul believes that he has been divinely set apart, and the primary objective of his apostolic activity is to preach the gospel among the Gentiles.[11] One may rightly ask: what is this gospel that Paul has been commissioned to proclaim?

Because in many instances the New Testament is "insider literature"—texts written by and for those who already believe in Christ—it often does not elaborate upon the definitions of terms and concepts it employs. Yet there is a rare moment in another Pauline missive, Rom 1:16-17, where Paul attempts to define the gospel.

In Rom 1:16-17 Paul suggests that the gospel is not so much an object as it is an event. He declares that the gospel is the "power of God" (δύναμις θεοῦ) through which God acts decisively to save those who have faith. Thus an apostle is one sent by Jesus to proclaim the gospel, and in the very act of proclaiming this good news the apostle believes that the event proclaimed is actually occurring and that the power of God is flowing through the apostle to achieve the purposes of God.[12]

In Gal 1:1, after immediately identifying himself as an apostle, Paul emphatically denies twice that human beings had anything to do with his apostolic identity and function. As an apostle, Paul has been the recipient of a powerful experience of God[13] and understands his work and preaching as media through which God's power flows. Paul's (apostolic) identity and function do not emanate from an authorizing consensus of a company of people. Thus he says that his apostleship did not come "from humans" (ἀπ᾽ ἀνθρώπων).

Nor did some influential person in the Christian community act as his patron while Paul served his "apostolic apprenticeship." Paul declares that his apostleship did not come "through a (specific) human" (δι' ἀνθρώπου). His authority and function originate in Jesus and in God. If a skeptic inquired of Paul concerning his apostolic credentials, the only thing that Paul could offer would be the testimony of his experience with Jesus and God, but for Paul that experience would be more than sufficient.

One should also note that Paul construes the relationship between God and Jesus functionally, or in terms of an experience. In v. 2 we are centuries away from the philosophical speculations concerning the ontological relationship between God and Jesus that would occupy the Church in its great christological debates.[14] For Paul the relationship between Jesus and God is best expressed in terms of an experience. God is the one who raised Jesus from the dead.

In the remainder of the abbreviated epistolary introduction in 1:3-5 Paul further underscores the centrality of experience in his understanding of the gospel. In v. 3 Paul offers the salutatory words of grace and peace to the Galatians. According to Walter Bauer, "In Christian epistolary literature from the time of Paul χάρις is found with the sense (divine) *grace* or *favor* in fixed formulas at the beginning and end of letters."[15] The word "peace" (εἰρήνη) is the Greek equivalent to the Hebrew *shalom* (שָׁלוֹם), which carries many nuances, including that of safety, soundness, and security.[16]

These words "grace" and "peace" have a long history of meaning for Jews, but what they mean for Paul in this context is expressed again in terms of experience and activity. This divine grace that Paul hopes the Galatians will not refuse results from and is manifested in the sacrificial giving of Jesus. In 1:4 Paul offers an appositional gloss on the phrase "the Lord Jesus Christ" that appears at the end of v. 3. Paul describes Jesus as one "who gave himself on behalf of our sins." A person cannot comprehend the profound meaning of grace apart from the act of receiving grace. For Paul, the act by which God demonstrated God's divine favor toward humanity most completely and convincingly was the sacrificial death of Jesus.[17] Therefore the first part of v. 4 can be seen as an explication of the meaning of "grace" in Paul's greeting in v. 3.

Furthermore, for Paul peace is not an abstract category but is the state that results from God's deliverance. To have peace is to be rescued from this present evil age. At this point Paul does not expand upon why he believes that the present age is evil. Perhaps the present predicament of the world is the consequence of "the elements of the world" (τὰ στοιχεῖα) mentioned in 4:3, which we shall discuss later.

For now the point is that peace is not some abstract absence of conflict and evil. Instead, peace is being rescued in the very midst of conflict
and evil. It is precisely the presence of conflict that highlights the mag-
nitude of the peace of God. This divine rescue operation is the purpose
of the sacrificial giving of Jesus. In v. 4 Paul begins the phrase about
Jesus rescuing us with the words "in order that" (ὅπως).[18] Therefore the
second part of v. 4 can be seen as an explication of the meaning of peace
in Paul's greeting in v. 3. Jesus' sacrificial death exemplifies the meaning
of grace. Jesus' "rescue operation" exemplifies the meaning of peace.

In Gal 1:6-9 Paul further underscores the importance of experience
as the basis of God's acceptance of the Gentiles. Not only is Paul utterly
astonished (θαυμάζω)[19] by the Galatians' desertion of the gospel to
another (pseudo) gospel; he considers those who advocate such a desertion to be persons who wish to pervert the gospel. The verb "to pervert"
(μεταστρέφω) can denote the change of one thing into its opposite.[20] In
Paul's estimation this is exactly what is happening and will continue to
happen if the Galatians leave the (true) gospel and cling to another
(pseudo) gospel.

In the gospel Christ called the Galatians in grace, and later we learn
that this was a call to freedom (Gal 5:13). But if the Galatians turn to
this (pseudo) gospel their freedom will metamorphose into a return to
slavery (Gal 4:9, 5:1). This (pseudo) gospel, apparently being proclaimed
by the messengers who are causing the confusion, would transform or
pervert freedom into its exact opposite—slavery. Therefore Paul curses
anyone proclaiming a gospel other than the true one. The scope of his
curse is wide enough to include both himself and the angels.

Evaluated by the rubric of African American experience, Paul offers
insights in Gal 1:1-9 that are both relevant and helpful to our quest for
liberation. Historically, African Americans have believed that the
essence and authenticity of one's life and calling neither arise from nor
depend ultimately upon the approval of a (white) person or a group of
(white) people but on an experience (of God).[21] This experience, as in
the case of Paul, may take the form of a "revelation," but the form and
content of the revelation will vary depending on the person and community.

Countless African American parents, preachers, educators, and activists throughout our history in the United States have tried heroically,
in the face of robust white supremacist ideology[22] to instill the belief in
their children that one's value does not ultimately depend on the approval of (white) people. This is a message that we must continually

preach to our African American children because they are constantly assailed by "the elements of the world." The validity of their lives has everything to do with their revelations or dreams of who they believe they are being called to be.

For one African American child the revelation might take the form of an impulse to be a renowned writer, and this revelation might come by means of reading the literature of Paul Laurence Dunbar or Alice Walker. For another child the revelation might be a dream of rising to national political prominence. This revelation might come from hearing the stories of the political trailblazing of Texas Congresswoman Barbara Jordan and of Virginia's former Governor, Douglas Wilder, the first African American governor in United States history.

So often, dominant white society has told African Americans, especially our children, that our specific callings or "apostleships" in life are invalid because those callings have not bowed at the altar of white society to pay homage and to receive permission to exist. If African Americans had waited for the validation of our callings and our lives by other people we would have perished, for so often the people from whom the validation would have come were opposed, for ideological reasons, to our very existence as a people.

Carlyle Fielding Stewart gives eloquent expression to the integral role of African American spirituality in helping black people articulate the "revelations" that validate their existence apart from the estimations of white culture. He writes:

> An objective of African American spirituality has been to instill in black people self-love, self-respect, a sense of justice, and equality rooted in divine love. Centering black people in an all-enveloping love of God has been a principal task of black spirituality. . . . The simple practice of love among black people comes from knowing unconditionally that God loves them. . . . It also means that no other people can ultimately wield the power or authority to determine black self-worth.[23]

African Americans have bypassed many of the practices and values of white America in favor of "a direct existential encounter with a higher power."[24] In some cases that higher power has been African American pride and gratitude to our ancestors; in other cases that higher power has been God. For African Americans, the freedom to have one's destiny in life validated by a higher power than people (i.e., white people) is one meaning of having a revelation "not from humans nor through a human, but through Jesus Christ and God the father."

Paul's emphasis upon experience and validation by a higher power squares existentially with aspects of African American experience.

Also in 1:3-4, Paul's comments on peace and on the rescue operation of Jesus may also illuminate African American experience. As discussed earlier, peace is not the overall *absence* of, but the *deliverance* in the midst of conflict and evil. In the resurrection of Jesus from the dead, which is God's "rescue operation" *par excellence,* the hopeful message is not the absence of, but rather the triumph over death. Divine rescue comes in the midst of struggle and conflict.

African Americans would do well to remember that divine rescue comes in the midst of struggle. Sadly, many young African Americans review the gains of the civil rights movement and feel as if struggle is no longer needed. How misguided these perceptions are. In our quest for liberation African Americans not only wrestle with flesh and blood, but we also struggle against the principalities and powers of deep-seated racism and xenophobia in the white American community. Insofar as God, or any other agent, is going to help us to rescue ourselves from oppression it will be a rescue in the very midst of struggle and conflict. In this present evil age ours is a struggle against powerful dominant groups. With clairvoyance, Frederick Douglass well over a century ago instructed African Americans that our peace would swoop in on the wings of struggle and political agitation of assorted varieties. Douglass sagaciously commented:

> If there is no struggle, there is no progress. Those who profess to favor freedom and yet deprecate agitation are men who want crops without plowing up the ground. They want rain without thunder and lightning. They want the ocean without the awful roar of its many waters. This struggle may be a moral one; or it may be physical one, and it may be both moral and physical, but it must be a struggle. Power concedes nothing without a demand. It never did and it never will.[25]

Finally, the curses that Paul utters on the agitators who are peddling another (pseudo) gospel are also relevant for African American experience. The gospel has called us to freedom. Thus any other gospel that transforms our freedom into slavery is a perversion and a pseudo gospel. In 1:8 Paul wishes that even a "messenger from heaven" (ἄγγελος ἐξ οὐρανοῦ) would be cursed or cut off if that messenger proclaimed a pseudo gospel.

In a similar vein African Americans would do well to follow Paul's courageous example of naming and cursing those messages and messengers who push a "gospel" that would pervert our liberty into bondage, even if those messengers comes from "high places" (e.g., the presidential administration, the halls of Congress, the Supreme Court, the media, and the entertainment industry). African Americans must begin to realize that some of the most menacing threats to our freedom have black, *not white,* faces.

Surely the great African and African American freedom fighters did not suffer, bleed, and die so that contemporary African Americans could parade around half-naked in music videos on television, promoting a culture of gratuitous violence and irresponsible and dangerous sexual activity. This example of the perversion of our freedom at the hands of segments of the entertainment industry is but one example of messengers in high places who may be leading us down perilous paths.

Other potentially dangerous (pseudo) messengers may be the so-called "prosperity" preachers, who are enormously popular in certain segments of African American Christian life. My main criticism is not of the teaching that prosperity is a part of God's promise to God's people. My contention is that these preachers inevitably reduce the expansive notion of prosperity simply to financial well-being. Then, when they talk about financial matters, they speak merely with respect to the individual and rarely, if ever, with a view to how African Americans corporately may pool our financial assets to address the systemic ills that blight our communities.

Paul's invocation of a curse upon those who participate in the mutation of freedom into slavery should remind African Americans that in our struggle we need more than "black faces in high places." The mere presence of "black faces in high places" does not necessarily insure that those faces will provide legislation or cultural productivity that will assist the liberation agenda.[26]

For a moment let me imagine what Paul's curse in Gal 1:9 upon the pseudo messengers of the "gospel" might sound like if it were run through the filter of twenty-first-century African American experience:

> Let politicians be cursed who enact legislation that runs counter to the needs of the larger African American community. In other words, we will not vote for you. Let entertainers be cursed who produce "art" that promotes self-hatred, violence, and sexual promiscuity. In other words, we will not buy your compact discs or visit the box offices where your movies play. Let preachers be cursed who are more concerned about building bigger churches than they are about building up the brokenhearted in the communities around their churches. In other words, we

will not tithe our money in your offering plates, nor frequent your halls of worship.

Maybe one of the most significant things that contemporary freedom fighters can learn from Paul in Gal 1:1-9 is that when the freedom of one's entire community hangs in the balance it may be appropriate from time to time to "curse" those who attempt to hinder the progress. I mean this, of course, not in the sense of *profane articulations*. Rather contemporary freedom fighters, who are concerned about the proliferation of pseudo messengers, must aggressively engage in *sacred actions* that may nullify the injurious effects of the pseudo gospel.

B. Galatians 2:1-10

1. Then, after fourteen years, again I came up to Jerusalem with Barnabas, taking along also Titus.
2. I came up on account of revelation, and I presented to them the gospel that I preach among the Gentiles. Privately, [I also presented the gospel that I preach][27] to those who were apparently the leaders, lest in some way I was running or had run in vain.
3. But not even Titus, a Greek person who was with me, was compelled to be circumcised.
4. But on account of false brothers who were smuggled in, who craftily came to scope out our freedom, which we have in Christ Jesus, in order that they might enslave us—
5. to whom not even for a moment did we submit in order that the truth of the gospel might remain for you.
6. From the people who appeared to be leaders (what sort of people they were made no difference to me. God does not show partiality) the ones seeming to be leaders added nothing to me.
7. But, on the contrary, when they saw that I had been entrusted with the gospel for the uncircumcised—just as Peter had been entrusted with the gospel for the circumcised—
8. for the one who worked in Peter for the apostleship for the circumcised worked also in me for the apostleship for the uncircumcised.
9. And when James, and Cephas, and John, the ones who were apparently the pillars, saw the grace that was given to me, they gave to me and to Barnabas the right hand of fellowship, in order that we might go to the Gentiles, and they to the circumcised.
10. They asked only one thing, that we remember the poor, a request that I was eager to fulfill.

As if the importance of his revelation from God was not sufficiently emphasized in Galatians 1, Paul continues in Galatians 2 to underscore the importance of this experience and of how this experience constitutes the basis of his apostolic authority. In Galatians 2 Paul recounts the salient events that transpired during his second visit to Jerusalem. In order to fully appreciate certain nuances of Paul's report of his second trip to Jerusalem we need to explore certain aspects of his first visit, which he discusses in Gal 1:18-20. Thus an interpretation of 2:1-10 must take into account factors from Galatians 1.

In 2:1 Paul writes: "Then, after fourteen years, again I came up to Jerusalem, with Barnabas, taking along also Titus." If we follow the chronology provided in Galatians 1–2, as many as seventeen years may have elapsed between Paul's initial revelation spoken of in 1:15-16 and the events recorded in 2:1-10. According to Paul, immediately after receiving his revelation of Jesus he went into Arabia and returned to Damascus.[28] Only then, after three years, did Paul go up to the Holy City to visit with Peter.

Paul's belief in his equal standing with the other apostles is evident in several places in Galatians 1–2. Paul declares in 1:16-17 that immediately after receiving this revelation he neither conferred with flesh and blood nor did he go up to Jerusalem to those who were apostles before him. The mention of his not conferring with flesh and blood certainly harks back to his repeated emphasis earlier in Gal 1:1 that human agency had nothing to do with the origin of his revelation or the means by which he received it.

In Gal 1:17 Paul indicates that during that first visit to Jerusalem the weight of history was on the side of the Jerusalem apostles. He acknowledges that those in Jerusalem were apostles before he was. These Jerusalem leaders had been commissioned as apostles before Paul's ministry began, and they were engaged in ministry on behalf of the risen Christ even during the period when Paul was vigorously seeking to destroy the Christian movement.[29] Moreover, Peter and James, whom he mentions in 1:18-19, could lay claim to having had actual encounters with Jesus during his earthly ministry.

Yet the very fact that Paul recognizes that history is on the side of the Jerusalem apostles only heightens his rejection of their superior status. This rejection is intimated by his declaration that he did not go *immediately* to Jerusalem. Furthermore, even when Paul did go to Jerusalem the first time he went merely to visit Peter. The visit lasted only fifteen days, and in that period the only other person he saw was James, the brother of the Lord. Paul was not seeking Peter's validation in this visit. As Hans Dieter Betz observes, "An informal 'visit' to the famous Cephas by the Apostle [Paul] is quite understandable after all these years, and it does not put into question the contention that he received the gospel from divine revelation and not from human sources."[30]

According to 2:1, fourteen years intervened between Paul's first visit to Jerusalem with Peter and the events of the Jerusalem Conference recounted in Gal 2:1-10. In 2:2 Paul states that his trip to Jerusalem was on account of revelation. By employing the phrase "on account of revelation" (κατὰ ἀποκάλυψιν) Paul may be engaging in yet another attempt to distance himself from the authority of the Jerusalem apostles.

He went to Jerusalem and laid before them the gospel that he had been preaching among the Gentiles and also presented his gospel to the so-called "Pillars"[31] in a private meeting. Paul did this so that he might not run in vain. At first glance it may seem that the phrase "lest in some way I was running or had run in vain" (μή πως εἰς κενὸν τρέχω ἢ ἔδραμον) is a veiled reference to Paul's actual dependence on the Jerusalem apostles, suggesting that Paul actually did go to Jerusalem to receive their approval and validation. This suggestion can be refuted on several counts.

First, Paul did not go to Jerusalem in order to seek approval so that he might continue preaching his version of the gospel among the Gentiles. He went to Jerusalem because he had been preaching this version of the gospel among the Gentiles for fourteen or more years. His purpose was to inform (and to persuade) those in Jerusalem. It is unlikely that after fourteen years of apostolic labor Paul would feel obliged to seek the permission and approval of the Jerusalem apostles to preach his circumcision-free gospel.

The second objection comes from Paul's words in 2:6. These apostles of repute did not intimidate Paul. Their reputation meant nothing to him because God shows no partiality. For Paul there could be no greater demonstration of God's impartiality than his being entrusted with the apostleship to the Gentiles. By means of his revelation and commission Paul was on equal ground with the Jerusalem apostles. Those who thought they were something added nothing to Paul.

The reader who is sensitive to nuance might hear a degree of mocking in Paul's language in 2:6. He does not affirm the status of the Jerusalem leadership unequivocally. He says that the persons to whom he was talking in Jerusalem "*appeared* to be leaders."[32] If one were to translate Paul's language in 2:6 in more contemporary terms, it might be rendered in this way: "Those who thought (perhaps inordinately) that they were something (i.e., big shots), or who appeared on the surface to be apostolic 'heavyweights' really had nothing to add to me because God was as active in my ministry as God was in their ministries."

I have offered tenable refutations to the suggestion that in 2:2 Paul is implicitly admitting his dependence on the Jerusalem apostles. Ostensibly Paul journeyed to Jerusalem not to gain validation from the Jerusalem leaders. Rather, having already been completely convinced of the validity of his ministry, he traveled to Jerusalem to create a unifying alliance with the Jerusalem church.

Had the Jerusalem church severely challenged Paul's (circumcision-free) gospel preached to the Gentiles, the potential for unity among the Jewish and Gentile branches of Christianity would have been significantly reduced. With an account of certain features of Paul's experiences in Jerusalem before us, we must now inquire how Paul's experiences in Jerusalem might offer useful analogues for African American liberation efforts.

Throughout our history in this country African Americans have been frequently accosted by certain white Americans who have (condescendingly) thought that their cultural norms were preeminent. These white people have negotiated relationships with African Americans as if white people were and would always be the benefactors and as if African Americans were and always would be the beneficiaries (of white intellectual and cultural largesse). Clearly, it has been thought that white culture has something to add to African American culture, but the possibility of mutual enrichment has been thought to be out of the question.

Acting as if theirs is the only culture and history that matters, some white Americans have surmised that those who stand outside their culture and history lack inherent validity and therefore must go to "Jerusalem" to receive white approval. Inherent in this invitation for African Americans to come to "Jerusalem" is the patronizing attitude that African American culture is insufficient.

It is precisely this assumption from which African Americans seek release—the assumption that authenticity and approval must come from "Jerusalem." This assumption explains how generations of Americans of many different cultural backgrounds have been taught in schools and universities a world history with little or no reference to the contributions of people of African descent.

In 1933 the eminent African American historian Carter G. Woodson lamented the lack of emphasis on African Americans in American education. He wrote: "Looking over the course of study of the public schools, one finds little to show that the Negro figures in these curricula."[33] Although some progress has been made since Woodson penned these words, far too many African American parents, educators, students, and community activists must still insist (and even protest) that African and African American resources become integral features of educational curricula. For example, the overarching "approval" of African American culture during "Black History Month" in February only throws into relief the larger dismissal and silence about our culture throughout the rest of the year.

On a personal note, as a biblical scholar I have extensive knowledge of Jewish and Greco-Roman culture, and this knowledge is indispensable for my critical engagement with the Bible. Yet I feel an abiding sense of shame that I know more about Israel, Greece, and Rome than I do about the continent from which my people (and all people) originated. One wonders whether Carter G. Woodson would say to me, "Brad, in spite of your considerable education, evidenced by your college degrees, there is another sense in which your *mis*-education is manifested by your relative ignorance of your own people."

On those occasions when the dominant culture refers to African American heritage these references have generally been made with respect to slavery and rarely to the creative genius, artistic prowess, life-affirming spirit, and considerable intellectual and cultural contributions of people of African descent. The history and experiences of African and African American societies have been considered inauthentic or unimportant because they do not come from "Jerusalem." Of course anything that has not come from "Jerusalem" and her apostles cannot be authentic, for "Jerusalem," in the dominant ideology, is the epicenter of authenticity.

The unabashed celebration and elevation of African American experience is our way of telling dominant culture that it is no longer necessary for us to come to "Jerusalem" to those who were apostles before us. We are as much apostles as they are, and we, too, have a history that validates our humanity and our culture. If we decide to go to "Jerusalem," we shall go of our own accord. We shall go not in order to be authenticated but precisely because we have been authenticated and are eager and proud to lay before those in "Jerusalem" the gospel of our liberation, which we have believed and which we are now preaching among ourselves.

Before continuing my discussion of the contemporary implications of Galatians 2 for African Americans I need to return momentarily to the ancient context. Paul goes to Jerusalem to explain his gospel to the apostles, perhaps with the hope of persuading them of its validity. From Paul's report in 2:7, his persuasive tactics were effective. After his presentation the Jerusalem apostles saw that Paul indeed had been entrusted with the "gospel for the uncircumcised." They also recognized that the God working in Peter was also the God working in Paul. What a powerful and far-reaching recognition this was!

As George Howard rightly surmises, "Paul's language in 2:1-10 reflects a theological implication inherent in Paul's gospel that the unity which was destined for the church was one which envisioned a continued ethnic and cultural distinction between the Jewish and Gentile wings of the Church."[34] According to Paul's understanding of the implications of the Jerusalem conference articulated in 2:7-10, Paul would lead the evangelistic campaign among the Gentiles, thus allowing Gentiles to enter the Church as Gentiles. Peter and others would lead the evangelistic campaign among the Jews, thus allowing the Jews to enter the Church as Jews.

A commitment to the gospel would not, of necessity, entail an obliteration of one's ethnic distinctiveness,[35] yet a commitment to one's ethnic distinctiveness would not, of necessity, obliterate the unity implied by the gospel. Though there were two evangelistic campaigns, there was still one gospel. Said another way, the Church would be filled with *Jewish* Christians and *Gentile* Christians, and the beauty of the gospel is that the acknowledgment of this diversity would not (or should not) eclipse the reality that Jewish and Gentile believers were all *Christians*.

If this is an accurate rendering of Paul's estimation of the Jerusalem conference, such a vision of unity accords nicely with the aims of black and womanist theologies and of an African American liberation movement, which include the creation of theological analysis and solutions that consider and speak to the present needs of African Americans. Many African Americans would share Paul's understanding of unity, namely that unity is not an antithesis (either/or) but rather a dialectic (both/and).

As discussed in Chapter One, the unity of the African American identity is not being either African or American, but being both at the same time. The dominant ideology has tried to resolve this energizing dialectic that fuels the African American spirit. On some occasions, as mentioned previously, white society has tried to prohibit us from being fully American. More recently, under the guise of a political liberalism that naïvely asserts that ethnic and racial differences are immaterial, dominant society has tried to encourage us not to be African.

To dominant society we declare unashamedly that we are Americans, and at the same time we are also *African* Americans. We are Christians, and we are also *black* Christians. And if one were to relate this way of thinking to the text of Galatians, Paul seems to say that the Galatians are Christians, and they are *Gentile* Christians.

Before proceeding any further I must offer a word concerning the traditional understanding of the agreement reached at the Jerusalem conference and also clarify the difference between what I perceive to be Paul's understanding of cultural distinction and a conventional African American understanding of cultural distinction.

Traditional scholarship often regards the agreement reached at the conference as a mere concession on the part of the Jerusalem apostles with respect to Paul's circumcision-free gospel. As Hans Dieter Betz notes, whether the position of the Jerusalem apostles was "theologically distinctive or a mere willingness to be broad-minded" cannot be decided.[36] Whether the Jerusalem apostles were embarking upon a new and distinct theological position by their concession or whether they were attempting to be broad-minded, it is unlikely that leaders of such prominence in the Christian community would have made this decision lightly.

Perhaps they were compelled by Paul's position. In some sense, by Jewish standards, the position of the conservative Jewish Christians, whom Paul calls "false brothers," was more "natural,"[37] or at least made complete sense. Yet not only did the Jerusalem apostles decide in favor of Paul's position; they also decided against the position of the "false brothers." Interpretations that refer to their actions as a mere concession might overlook the possibility that the Jerusalem apostles were compelled at the level of theological principle by Paul's argument.

Insofar as Paul championed the right of Gentile Christianity to exist, he was in some way advocating a cultural distinction between Jews and Gentiles. Yet Paul's understanding of cultural distinction is possibly narrower than the understanding of cultural distinction that an African American liberation agenda might affirm. By proclaiming a gospel of uncircumcision Paul was helping in some limited way to establish a Gentile Christian identity. The Gentile believer was a Christian, but was not a Jewish Christian. Paul was thus encouraging the Gentile believers to say "no" to the dominant ideology of the Judaizers,[38] but he does not appear to be encouraging them to say "yes" to Gentile culture *per se*. Paul's assessment of cultural distinction could be described as a "negative" understanding, namely one that defined Gentile identity by what it was *not*.

A liberating understanding of African American identity and cultural distinctiveness should, I contend, be fuller. Although it should contain the "negative" understanding seen in Paul, it should also have a "positive" understanding, which Paul lacks. African Americans should desire not only to say "no" to dominant white culture but also to say "yes" to black culture.

Blackness as an identity is not merely the negation of "whiteness"; it is also an affirmation of "blackness." Paul planted the seed of the necessity of cultural distinction in the Church. African Americans should water the seed. The abundant harvest for which we pray will be an affirmation among African Americans of our culture and history alongside our commitment to God's actions in Christ. In principle, African Americans and Paul have a relatively similar understanding of unity. Unity does not presuppose uniformity. But as a result of the pressing need for affirmation among African Americans, a new and more liberating understanding of Christian unity may be needed—one that does not view ethnic distinctiveness and Christian identity as mutually exclusive. The similarities between Paul's version of unity and the African American version will be noted in the following interpretations, but the difference must be borne in mind as well.

C. Galatians 2:11-21

11. But when Cephas came to Antioch I opposed him to his face, because he was condemned.

12. Before certain people from James came, he was eating regularly with the Gentiles. But when they came he began withdrawing and separating himself, because he was fearing the circumcision party.

13. And the other Jews acted hypocritically along with him, such that even Barnabas was swept up in their hypocrisy.

14. But when I saw that they were not walking correctly towards the truth of the gospel, I said to Cephas in the presence of everyone, "If you, being a Jew, live as a Gentile and not as a Jew, how can you compel Gentiles to live as Jews?"

15. We, who are Jews by birth and not from the Gentile sinners,

16. know that a person is not justified from the works of the law except through the faith of Jesus Christ. And we believed in Christ Jesus in order that we might be justified by the faith of Christ and not from the works of the law, because from the works of the law no flesh will be justified.

17. But if, seeking to be justified in Christ, we ourselves have been found to be sinners, is Christ a servant of sin? Absolutely not!

18. For if I build up again the very things that I destroyed, I present myself as a transgressor.

19. For I through the law died to the law, in order that I might live to God. I have been crucified with Christ.

20. It is no longer I who live, but Christ lives in me; and the life I now live in the flesh, I live in faith—faith in the Son of God who loved me and gave himself for me.

21. I do not nullify the grace of God. For if justification is through the law, then Christ died for no reason.

The right hand of fellowship extended by the "Pillar Apostles" to Paul and Barnabas in Jerusalem suggested that the "Pillar Apostles" accepted this emerging concept of Christian unity implicit in the evangelistic division (Gal 2:7-9). George Howard remarks, "For Yahweh to be the God of all . . . the Jews had to accept the Gentiles as they were, uncircumcised, and the Gentiles had to accept the Jews as they were, circumcised."[39] Otherwise God would not be a universal God but only the God of the Jews. Possibly it was with this understanding of unity and inclusion that Paul, Barnabas, and Titus left Jerusalem to continue preaching their gospel of uncircumcision.

In Paul's estimation the Jerusalem conference affirmed that there was one gospel, but it was elastic enough to permit important ethnic distinctions to remain in force among the Jews and the Gentiles insofar as those distinctions posed no threat to the fellowship of Jews and Gentiles. The exigencies of actual communal life would soon put to the test the strength of the agreement reached at Jerusalem.

In 2:11-14 Paul narrates an episode that occurs at some unspecified time after the Jerusalem meeting. Peter comes to Antioch,[40] an important early Christian center where Gentile converts were not compelled to be circumcised in order to become Christians. According to Paul, while in Antioch Peter ate regularly with the Gentiles.[41] The agreement reached earlier in Jerusalem had focused ostensibly on the issue of circumcising Gentile converts to Christianity. Peter's action in Antioch signaled that the Jewish dietary laws, which could also prohibit fellowship among Jews and Gentiles, could be repealed in the service of unity.

Yet, when representatives from Jerusalem ("certain people from James," 2:12) came to Antioch, Peter withdrew and separated himself.[42]

Following Peter's lead, Barnabas and other Jews who had been sharing table fellowship with the Gentiles separated themselves from Paul and the rest of the Gentiles. Paul indicted all those who withdrew on the charge of hypocrisy. What triggered this indictment from Paul?

An analysis of some of the terms Paul uses to describe the event might provide insight. According to Hans Dieter Betz, the verb "to withdraw" is "highly polemical and is taken from the arsenal of military and political language . . . [and] occurs as a description of military and political maneuvers of retreating into an inconspicuous or sheltered position."[43] Betz also notes that the verb "to separate," coupled with the pronoun "himself" (ἑαυτόν) is "a Jewish technical term describing cultic separation from the 'unclean.'"[44] With a fuller understanding of these important terms we may be better equipped to understand Paul's volatile reaction to Peter's action.

In Paul's estimation Peter's (regular) table fellowship with the Gentile converts at Antioch provided *social* expression to the *theological* reality, namely that in service of the unity of the gospel Jewish boundary markers that had imposed barriers between Jews and Gentiles would not be required of Gentile believers. At the meeting in Jerusalem the specific Jewish boundary marker decided upon was circumcision.

According to James D. G. Dunn, Paul, when assessing Peter's actions as hypocritical, may have extended the boundaries of the agreement in Jerusalem to include the food laws. Dunn observes, "On Paul's side, the agreement at Jerusalem [concerning the dispensability of circumcision for Gentiles] was probably taken as a point of principle. . . . The agreement in Jerusalem would be understood by him as providing a precedent for playing down other boundary-defining, Gentile excluding commandments."[45]

Insofar as Peter had been eating with the Gentiles, thereby recognizing their justification, his withdrawal from the Gentiles when representatives from James came could be construed as a tacit denial of that justification. Peter would only need to withdraw from the Gentiles if he believed them to be ritually impure or unclean. Their inclusion into God's family by means of their justification by Christ surely had removed from them that unclean status, or had it (for Peter)?

We can never fully know all the events surrounding the Antioch incident, but one credible reconstruction may be that Paul had thought through the implications of the Jerusalem agreement "too much" and Peter had thought through the implications "too little." Dunn speaks to the fact that Paul may have extended the Jerusalem conference's specific agreement about circumcision to a larger principle. Thus Paul contributed to the debacle at Antioch by making too much of the Jerusalem agreement. What do I mean when I say Peter had thought through the Jerusalem agreement "too little"?

The Jerusalem agreement was a statement of Christian unity. Jewish Christians and Gentile Christians were to be united by their belief in God's action in Christ, yet their belief in Christ did not necessitate an abandonment of their cultural distinctions. With respect to circumcision such an understanding of unity would work in the following manner. Jewish Christians should continue to be circumcised insofar as circumcision was a social custom that distinguished them as Jews. By the same token, circumcision should not be enjoined upon Gentile Christians insofar as uncircumcision was a social custom that distinguished Gentiles.

As Dunn noted above, even though the specific agreement at the Jerusalem conference involved only circumcision, Paul ostensibly extended this line of reasoning in the Antioch incident and applied it to the food laws as well. When Paul applied his way of thinking to the *food laws,* this possibly would have produced considerable complication for concrete expressions of Christian unity in Antioch. A word of explanation is in order.

Even though a Jewish male was circumcised in order to keep the covenant and to distinguish himself from Gentiles, the reality of one's circumcision might not be regularly detected. For example, only if one were exercising nude in the gymnasium in a Greco-Roman city might one's circumcision be noticed. Thus one might adopt this important Jewish boundary marker without necessarily precluding social interaction with uncircumcised Gentiles.

Ostensibly, in an early Christian community in the Diaspora[46] a Jewish Christian could decide to emphasize his Jewish heritage by submitting to circumcision, and a Gentile Christian could emphasize his Gentile heritage by refusing circumcision. And in spite of these important cultural stances there could be unity among Jewish and Gentile Christians in that community. In other words, circumcision and uncircumcision could still be maintained as social, even ethnic boundary markers. Some of the meanings of such markers would simply have been reconceptualized.[47]

Accordingly, in Antioch and in Paul's churches in Galatia the Jewish identity of one Christian and the Gentile identity of another Christian would not have been obliterated or amalgamated into some universal identity. On the other hand, neither would one's Jewish or Gentile status have been the preeminent identity marker.

Believers' positions and identities in the world would always have been kept in tension with their identity as Christians, and that Christian identity would unite across social boundaries, not necessarily eliminate them. Given the more "hidden" nature of circumcision, social interaction between Jewish and Gentile Christians could have occurred much more openly. The food laws, another important Jewish requirement whose result was to separate Jews from Gentiles, was a more "public" (i.e., open) social custom. It may have been more challenging to effect an approach to Christian community, which affirmed diversity within unity, in light of the food laws. Further clarification concerning the challenge to Christian unity posed by the food laws may be helpful.

Steven Fine, an orthodox Jew and an expert on synagogue practices in the Second Temple period, recently suggested to me that many theories surrounding the origin of the food laws miss the point. Some theories attempt to locate the origin of the food laws in hygienic purposes. Certain scholars argue that Jews did (and do) not eat particular foods because these foods might potentially carry disease. According to Fine, such an explanation eclipses a fundamental aspect of the food laws, which was (and is) to distinguish the Jews as people set apart by God.

Lester Grabbe bolsters Fine's observations. Concerning the food laws Grabbe writes:

> Just as the Israelites were not to eat certain animals, they were not to mix with other nations. The dietary regulations had both a practical and symbolic function; symbolically they stood for the fact that Israel was to keep itself free from intercourse with non-Israelites; practically, prohibition of eating certain animals meant that Jews could not socialize with those who ate these animals.[48]

The food laws gave tangible, ritual, and regular expression to the principle that Jews were to maintain their separateness from Gentiles. Thus when one attempted to affirm one's Jewish identity by keeping the food laws, this involved withdrawing, to some extent, from the Gentiles. A subtle "Catch 22" was created when the Jewish food laws and the principle of Christian unity advocated by the Jerusalem conference collided with one another.

If Jewish Christians wanted to maintain their Jewish identity by means of the food laws, they could not eat with Gentiles. But if Jewish Christians categorically refrained from fellowship with Gentile Christians simply because they were Gentiles, such action might potentially refute in *practice* the overarching *principle* of the Jerusalem agreement, namely that in spite of cultural differences Jewish and Gentile believers were united in one gospel and by one God. Possibly Peter and Paul had not sufficiently sorted out for themselves, and for the community, these subtle tensions prior to the arrival in Antioch of the representatives from James.

In an attempt to foster unity with the Gentiles, Peter may have shared table fellowship with them, actually relinquishing that part of his Jewish heritage that defined being Jewish in terms of prohibiting table fellowship with Gentiles. Those from James may not have shared this freedom and may have pressured Peter into a more traditional understanding of his Jewish identity. Consequently, Peter withdrew from sharing at table with the Gentiles at Antioch.

The above reconstruction attempts to offer a more "generous" or sympathetic reading of Peter, so that Peter does not appear to be a completely fickle person who wavers under the political pressure of the moment. Notwithstanding attempts to honor the tensions that may have been prevalent at Antioch, one can also see how Paul may have interpreted Peter's action as a serious breach of Christian unity.

From Paul's standpoint Christ had nullified old ethnic stereotypes[49] about the inherent uncleanness of Gentiles. Thus to the degree that Jewish practices of separation from the Gentiles were founded upon those stereotypes, those practices of separation would have to be reexamined or, in some cases, even abolished. If one held on to those practices of separation, even at the cost of destroying Christian unity, one indicated a desire to be justified by the "works of the law" (i.e., Jewish boundary markers) rather than by the sacrificial death of Christ that was designed to benefit all who believed in it.

Since Peter had been eating with the Gentiles, thereby recognizing their justification by God, his separation from them simply because they were Gentiles, when those from James arrived, symbolized a reintroduction of problematic understandings of social identity. For Peter to withdraw himself from these Gentile Christians as if they were impure was to deny, in some fundamental way, that these Gentiles had in fact been justified by God *as Gentiles*.

For Paul such action, especially on the part of Peter and Barnabas who were present at the Jerusalem conference, was not consistent with the truth of the gospel. When he withdrew and separated himself from the Gentiles, after having dined with them, Peter indicated that he was a "play-actor," or one who pretended to be one thing when, in reality, he was another.

In short, Peter was a hypocrite (ὑποκριτής),[50] and his hypocrisy came at the moment of truth—a critical juncture when, by standing up for his convictions in the face of opposition, he could have sided with the disenfranchised Gentiles. If I may employ language from Chapter One of this book, Peter missed a prime opportunity to become "black," or at least to identify with some of the "black" condition. Thus even if one desires to give Peter the benefit of the doubt and consider the entire Antioch incident a case of miscommunication and misunderstanding, an African American reading of this event might contend that Paul still had justifiable grounds for his stern rebuke of Peter.

Possibly Peter was interested in practically exploring this concept of unity implicit in the Jerusalem agreement, whereby cultural differences were to be maintained. Therefore he shared table fellowship with the Gentiles, perhaps listening and learning about their experience of God in Christ. But when the possibility of oppression, unpopularity, and loss of political clout confronted Peter in the form of representatives from James, Peter's interest in the Gentiles' experience rapidly disappeared. According to Paul in 2:12, Peter withdrew to a sheltered position (ὑπέστελλεν).[51]

In the moment of truth Peter's real colors came shining through. To separate himself from the Gentiles as if they were unclean may have suggested that Peter was not *really* interested in understanding and appreciating the differences between Jews and Gentiles. When faced with the opportunity to stand with the marginalized group and suffer with them and even for them, Peter demonstrated that he would rather take refuge in the dominant ideology, which castigated Gentiles as persons who categorically stood outside of God's approval.

Paul's words in 2:14 indicate that he perceived Peter's action as an unwillingness to explore genuine unity. Paul accuses: "If *you*, being a Jew, live as a Gentile and not as a Jew, how can you compel Gentiles to live as Jews?" Although in his rebuke Paul is obviously angry, we may be able to detect traces of his understanding of the proper process by which unity in the Church may occur.

Peter was a Jew. He knew it, and the Gentiles knew it. Yet in the very act of eating with them Peter was making an earnest attempt to learn about their ways and customs from their perspective, no longer being satisfied with ethnocentric myths about how all Gentiles were unclean. By emphasizing Peter's Jewishness ("If *you*,[52] being a Jew . . ." 2:14),

Paul is indicating that it is impossible for Peter to make the complete transition into being a Gentile. Peter cannot completely make this transition because by definition he is a Jew. If the Gentiles had required Peter to ignore completely his Jewish heritage, this, too, would have been an act of oppression and a breach of the concept of unity. Peter, however, could have tried to build bridges with the Gentiles.

From an African American perspective, genuine unity encourages one to be proud of one's heritage while sympathetically trying to learn about, not denigrate and obliterate, the heritages of other people. At the moment when Peter pulled away from the Gentiles simply because they were Gentiles he implicitly denigrated the Gentiles. Even if Peter's withdrawal from them did not actually imply that he thought Gentiles were unclean, his actions symbolically conveyed that the Gentiles were, indeed, outside the boundaries of God's approval.

African American history is replete with contemporary analogies to the Antioch event. Repeatedly African Americans have seen "play-actors" who, with their silver tongues and rehearsed actions, have espoused in the public square principles of racial unity and economic development. In the frenzy, for instance, of a political campaign they talk of building bridges to and coalitions with groups who are outside the power structure. They shake hands and eat with thousands of potential African American voters, promising better housing, an increase in the quality of life and education, and a decrease in police brutality in our communities. In order to secure votes these "play-actors" make an effort to know black people, and it even appears that they are trying as much as possible to be black people.

Yet so often, when the time has come to make good on these promises or to offer moral support to those on the fringes and to stand on the side of fairness and genuine unity these "play-actors" have withdrawn to a sheltered and inconspicuous political position. They have separated themselves from the now "unclean" African American community. Such actions expose a lack of interest in genuine unity and an unwillingness to risk privilege and power for the sake of racial reconciliation and community uplift.

Had they shown a willingness to stand up for the African American community in the moment of truth and to risk their position and privilege, though they had white skin, many in the African American community would have considered them to be "black" in some limited way and would have been even more willing to support them. But since the play-actors were not willing to take the risk they, much like Nicodemus, showed their unwillingness to be "black."[53] Whenever and wherever African Americans see such hypocrisy we, like Paul, must be willing to oppose it to its very face!

When a white person shows a genuine interest in the liberation of African Americans and lends support to the cause many African Americans are grateful to but somewhat leery of that person. African Americans may be skeptical for reasons such as those demonstrated in Antioch. Occasionally even the best-intentioned white Americans, who have been zealously committed to the cause of liberation, have withdrawn at the moment of truth—when things became too difficult or risky—and have separated, and no longer identified with the "black" condition.

Whether one sides with Peter or with Paul, the incident at Antioch reveals that from its earliest days the Church has struggled to translate its vaunted principle of "diversity in unity" into concrete practices. The many failures in Christian history to embody this principle should not dissillusion us about the possibilities but rather should galvanize us to continue pursuing this lofty and worthwhile goal. If the contemporary Church were to even approximate this principle in its practices, the many failures of the past would seem like an insignificant tax to pay for so large a benefit.

In 2:15-21 Paul's rebuke of Peter continues. Scholars have often debated where in the text the Antioch scene ends and Paul's editorial comments begin. Yet many would agree with James Dunn that in 2:15-21 Paul is not giving a verbatim report of his comments to Peter but rather is "echoing the line of argument, which he tried to develop on that occasion."[54] Galatians 2:15-21 contains some of the most crucial insights of the whole letter, and before dealing with these verses I must state some important assumptions that will guide my interpretation of this section.

First, Gal 2:15-21 is not some free-floating theological musing by Paul but rather insights intricately related to the "theme of inclusion of the uncircumcised Gentiles into the kingdom of God."[55] Second, following the assertion that has been made vogue by New Testament scholars such as Krister Stendahl[56] and E. P. Sanders,[57] I believe that Paul's problem with the law was *not* its supposed inability to be fulfilled.

The third assumption, which accords nicely with an African American insistence that biblical interpretation have social relevance, is that in 2:15-21 Paul's assertions are as much *social* as they are *doctrinal*. James Dunn is right when he emphasizes the social dimensions of Paul's attitude toward the law and of his teaching about circumcision. Dunn remarks, "Unless this social, we may even say national and racial, dimension of the issues confronting Paul is clearly grasped, it may well be nigh impossible to achieve an exegesis of Paul's treatment of the law."[58] With these assumptions in place I now turn to Gal 2:15-21.

Due to the complexity of Gal 2:15-21, and especially of 2:16, breaking v. 16 into four distinct clauses will facilitate this discussion.[59] I will assign each clause a letter:

> 16a: [We] know that a person is not justified from the works of the law except through the faith of Jesus Christ.
>
> 16b: And we believed in Christ Jesus
>
> 16c: in order that we might be justified by the faith of Christ and not from the works of the law,
>
> 16d: because from the works of the law, no flesh will be justified.

In 2:15-16 Paul refers to a concept that presumably Peter as a fellow Jew would have understood. By using the phrase "we who are Jews by birth" Paul appeals to the common heritage that he shares with Peter. In some sense what Paul is about to tell Peter is not novel. Peter knows[60] (εἰδότες) the conviction about to be espoused. The conviction is the Jewish belief that no person is justified from the works of the law. In other words, Jews knew that justification, the state of being in a proper covenant relationship with God and thereby being God's people, was ultimately a result of God's gracious initiative.

Jews fulfilled these works of the law mentioned in 2:16 not in order to earn God's favor but precisely as a sign that God's favor had been graciously given in a covenant and that the Jews desired to stay in the covenant. As E. P. Sanders remarks, "The intention and effort to be obedient [to the works of the law] constitute the *condition for remaining in the covenant,* but they do not *earn* it."[61] When Paul here speaks of works of the law, he generally has in mind "covenant works, works done in obedience to the law of the covenant."[62]

In particular these covenant works were thought to include circumcision, food, and Sabbath regulations that functioned, to use James Dunn's term, as "identity markers."[63] Dunn writes, "For the typical Jew . . . it would be virtually impossible to conceive of participating in God's covenant, and so in God's covenant righteousness, apart from these observances, these works of the law."[64] To participate in God's covenant was to be declared righteous, which does not "imply perfection but faithfulness."[65] The reality that justification was by *faith* was a Jewish understanding.

Paul and Peter, however, are not just Jews; they are Jewish Christians, and this is evident in the words of Gal 2:16a: [We] "know that a person is not justified from the works of the law except (ἐὰν μὴ) through the faith of Jesus Christ." As long as the works of the law are understood in the context of the Christ event (faith of Jesus Christ),[66] then such works are not inherently antithetical to the Christ event. No Jew would have thought that works of the law impugned God's grace. Thus it was possible for Jewish Christians to continue doing works of the law without nullifying the grace of God manifest in the Christ event. In 2:16 Paul is possibly closer to Peter than some have realized. As Jews, Paul and Peter understood that justification was on the basis of the gracious election of God. But as Jewish Christians they believed that God, in the Christ event, had made a new and a once-and-for-all demonstration of grace and election.

We should understand the phrase "the faith of Jesus Christ" in 2:16a as an abbreviation for the "Christ event." Moreover, we should translate 2:16a as "[we] know that a person is not justified from the works of the law *except* through the faith *of* Jesus Christ." Thus Paul in 2:16 is not repeating himself but suggesting how, in fact, people come to realize or "activate" the Christ event in their lives.[67] One "activates" the saving power of the Christ event (i.e., the faith *of* Jesus Christ) by faith *in* Jesus Christ.

In other words, God has provided the means for human salvation through the person and deeds of Jesus. Jesus faithfully carried out God's providential plan. Humans may become a part of that plan by investing belief in Jesus' person and deeds. This is what Paul means in 2:16c when he says, "And we believed *in* Christ Jesus. . . ."

Thus Paul can conclude that when persons invest belief in the Christ event they are justified by the Christ event ("faith of Jesus Christ" 2:16c) "and not from the works of the law because from the works of the law no flesh will be justified." By quoting and interpreting Ps 143:2 in Galatians 2:16d[68] Paul demonstrates that for the Jew (and the Jewish Christian) the works of the law never were thought to be the means to justification. Grace made operative through faith had always been the deciding factor, even before the Christ event.

Only when filtered through the Christ event can works of the law be a complement to faith, but when works of the law are absolutized and divorced from faith, then the law generally and the works of the law specifically will encourage "a sense of national superiority and presumption of divine favor."[69] Such presumption limits and nullifies the

grace of God since grace can be the possession of any person who in-
vests faith in Christ, regardless of ethnicity, social status, and gender.

With this said, perhaps we have stumbled across another reason for
Paul's rebuke of Peter. Not only did Peter show himself to be a play-
actor uninterested in genuine unity, but also by compelling the Gentiles
to abide by Jewish regulations Peter was implicitly denying the suffi-
ciency and universality of the Christ event to justify people. By withdrawing from the Gentiles at Antioch, Peter instead was (symbolically)
insisting that covenant acceptance by God could only come under the
rubric of Jewish practice and understanding of faith.

In the midst of this very complex passage African Americans should
still see the importance of experience as a basis for acceptance by God.
In Christianity the precondition for being in a covenant relationship
with God is an experience, namely the Christ event. One enters into that
covenant by means of faith, which is the experience of submitting one's
life to the sovereignty of God, Christ, and the Spirit[70] and conducting
one's life in ways that reflect that submission. Thus whereas the Christ
event is an enduring reality that traverses social barriers, the experience
or manifestations of investing faith in Christ will vary according to individual and communal norms. A manifestation of faith is valid insofar
as it does not nullify the very universal grace upon which the covenant
is based. Various social "identity markers" certainly have their place in
the expression or experience of faith, but they must be used with a sense
of openness. Let me solidify my point.

Christians worship God not to earn God's favor but because we
have received God's favor. Worship can be considered a manifestation of
Christian faith. When we gather to worship we are submitting to the
lordship of Christ and receiving instruction in and inspiration for
modes of living that reflect our submission.

If worship is a manifestation of faith in Christ, then traditional
African American Christian worship,[71] with its rhythmic music, ecstatic
dancing, and fervent preaching, as long as it comes from faith, is as valid
a manifestation of faith as is "high-church" liturgical worship with its
emphasis on the sacraments. For high-church Catholics or Protestants
to tell African American Baptists or Pentecostals that African American
worship is ineffectual and not pleasing to God is tantamount to saying
that God is a white Catholic or Protestant God who delights only in
high liturgy. Such a God would not be a universal God. The claiming
and owning of social particularities as means to express one's faith in
Christ is legitimate. In some sense it is precisely in the (healthy and

magnanimous) claiming of our particularities, not the ignoring or obliteration of them, that we truly begin to approximate the vastness of God.

In my professorial and pastoral vocations I have been heavily invested in various ecumenical dialogues—both interdenominational discussions among Christians and interfaith conversations between Jews and Christians. A particular frustration that I have had with some interdenominational discussions is that "ecumenism" is often, unfortunately, translated to mean "the bland wiping away of the very particularities that demonstrate how creative God is in fashioning us." On the contrary, I have always understood ecumenism to be the attempt to celebrate our *diversity*—which adds color and texture to our unity—and the attempt to celebrate our *unity*—which insures that our diversity will never mutate into provincialism.

In a recent article J. Frederick Holper explores how certain mainline white Christian traditions may learn from the examples of vital worship offered by certain other traditions that are rapidly growing. He cites as two of his examples African American congregations in Chicago (Trinity United Church of Christ[72] and St. Benedict the African Roman Catholic Church). He suggests that in both congregations the owning of social particularity in worship—manifested in the unashamed affirmation of Afrocentrism—enhances the worshipers' encounter with God. Writing as a Presbyterian and (largely) to Presbyterians, Holper asserts:

> Many of our EuroAmerican congregations wrongly assume that Presbyterians instinctively share a single culture. We need to develop a "practical" Reformed tradition of worship in conversation with the distinctive cultures and subcultures where our churches are planted. Our racial ethnic congregations might profitably serve as our tutors in the project. They've known all along that not every Presbyterian loves bagpipes.[73]

Holper's observations identify the longstanding African American spiritual reality that social identity and spiritual identity are and should be mutually reinforcing. Ironically, however, Holper's choice of language betrays one of the subtle yet significant obstacles that white Americans will need to overcome in order to make progress in the whole area of race relations. He contends that "our *racial ethnic* congregations" may be good tutors. My immediate question is: Are Afrocentric congregations the only ones that have a race or ethnicity? Because European American identity is so much the norm in the United States, race and ethnicity for many white people become "things" that "other people" have.

Bill Bradley, the former United States senator and presidential candidate who has long championed racial justice, has also noted the subtle assumption in white culture that race is something that "other" people have. He remarked:

> The hardest thing to get across is that whites have race, too. If you ask that same group [of people who attend political town meetings and discuss affirmative action], well, how many of you who are white think you have white-skin privilege? They look at you—What? What is white-skin privilege? It is taken for granted, a kind of privilege that most African Americans or Latinos or Asian Americans can never take for granted.[74]

Could it be that Paul and Peter's dispute at Antioch and my theological interpretation of it are indications of the dangers of taking cultural assumptions and privileges for granted? If we are interested in genuine reconciliation and fellowship across social lines that neither impugn God's universality nor obliterate our particularity we must unearth our deepest assumptions about ourselves and about others. Those assumptions and practices that foster fellowship across social boundaries and yet inculcate a strong sense of (group) identity should be maintained. Those assumptions and practices that foster a strong sense of (group) identity, but at the expense of fellowship across social boundaries, must be seriously reexamined, reconfigured, and possibly even abolished.

D. Galatians 3:1-5

1. O foolish Galatians! Who has bewitched you? Before your eyes Jesus Christ was publicly proclaimed as crucified.
2. I want to learn only this from you: From the works of the law did you receive the Spirit or from hearing and believing (the gospel)?[75]
3. How can you be so foolish? Having begun in the Spirit, are you now ending in the flesh?
4. Have you experienced so great a thing in vain, if it really was in vain?
5. Therefore, does God, who supplies to you the Spirit and works miracles among you, do this because of the works of the law or because of (your) hearing and believing (the gospel)?[76]

As we leave the Antioch incident Paul says that if the Gentiles begin abiding by Jewish regulations, especially circumcision, they will abandon their indigenous manifestation of covenant faith. In Paul's view such an abandonment would not only be foolish but tantamount to being bewitched. Thus Paul shouts in 3:1: "O foolish Galatians! Who has bewitched you? Before your eyes Jesus Christ was publicly proclaimed as crucified."

The Gentiles "knew from their own experience that their enjoyment of that promise [i.e., God's covenant promise discussed in 3:7ff] had not depended and would not depend on their aligning themselves visibly and physically with the native Jew by embracing the ancestral customs of the Jews."[77] The Gentile enjoyment of the covenant promises, here certified by the reception of the Holy Spirit, did not derive from Jewish works of the law, but came as a result of their hearing and believing the gospel proclamation. Throughout 3:1-5 Paul asks rhetorical questions to remind the Galatians of their experience. To have begun in the spirit but to end in *the flesh,* which undoubtedly is a sarcastic reference to circumcision, is foolishness and a manifestation of being bewitched.

I, and many African Americans, understand and share Paul's anguish and exasperation. Some of my fellow African Americans have been bewitched into believing that in order to have dignity and to be accepted they have to identify with white Americans not only ideologically, but even physically. Whereas the case at issue for us is not circumcision,[78] African American history is replete with alarming phenomena similar to the situation in Galatia.

Having fallen prey to the dominant ideology, certain African Americans have felt the need to look like white Americans physically, undergoing surgery and cosmetic procedures to thin out their lips and noses and to lighten their skin tones.[79] Interestingly, "high profile" African Americans, such as entertainers, have often submitted to these surgical procedures. One example is the internationally renowned African American music superstar Michael Jackson. No one knows all the circumstances surrounding his many cosmetic surgeries, but I am not alone in feeling that many of those surgeries were attempts to erase his black features as much as possible, thus making him more acceptable to white culture.[80]

Such actions by African Americans, especially those of public prominence, have contributed to the creation of whole generations of African Americans who are ashamed of their black skin and culture.[81] I am moved to ask these questions of those who have undergone such procedures: "Are you so foolish? Having begun as an African American with black skin, a broad nose, and thick lips, will you end as a white person with white skin, a thin nose, and slender lips? Are not such 'surgeries' a denial of grace? God made us as we are, and by our faith God accepts us into covenant relationship as we are."

E. Galatians 3:6-14

> 6. Just as Abraham "believed God, and it was reckoned to him as righteousness."
>
> 7. Be very certain,[82] therefore, that people of faith—these are the children of Abraham.
>
> 8. And the scripture, foreseeing that God would justify the Gentiles by faith, proclaimed ahead of time the good news to Abraham: "All the Gentiles will be blessed in you."
>
> 9. So that people of faith are blessed with Abraham the faithful.
>
> 10. For all who rely on the works of the law are under a curse. For it is written, "Cursed is everyone who does not remain in all the things written in the book of the law, to do them."
>
> 11. It is clear that no one is justified before God by the law because (the scripture says),[83] "The righteous person will live by faith."
>
> 12. But the law is not by faith, but (the scripture says),[84] "The one who does them will live by them."
>
> 13. Christ has redeemed us from the curse of the law by becoming a curse for us—for it is written, "Cursed is everyone who hangs upon a tree"—
>
> 14. in order that in Christ Jesus the blessing of Abraham might come to the Gentiles, so that we might receive the promise of the Spirit through faith.

After chiding the Galatians in 3:1-5 for having been bewitched by the dominant ideology, Paul in 3:6-14 takes his readers on a whirlwind excursion across the terrain of various biblical texts. The purpose of the excursion is to substantiate that God had always intended justification to be on the basis of faith and that God from the very beginning had the Gentiles in mind when the promise was given. In this section one can see Paul's fascinating attempt to transform the dominant ideology into a weapon of resistance.

Reading the opening words of Gal 3:6, one realizes that Paul has chosen as his point of departure an example that, on the surface, appears to support the dominant ideology. He begins his argument for the inclusion of the Gentiles with Abraham and quotes from Gen 15:6. This hardly seems like a judicious choice since the Jews hailed Abraham as a hero and a great man of faith. For the Jews the faith of Abraham spoken of in Gen 15:6 was "coupled with his acceptance of circumcision as referred to in the covenant of Gen 17:4-14."[85] Thus Paul begins with Abraham, a figure who may have been the example *par excellence* of the Judaizers.[86] Yet Paul's purpose is to use Abraham as a springboard into the transformation of the dominant ideology.

In 3:6 Paul suggests that Abraham's justification ultimately rested on God's activity. Grammatically, the phrase in 3:6b, "and it was reckoned to him as righteousness" (καὶ ἐλογίσθη αὐτῷ εἰς δικαιοσύνην) constitutes what New Testament scholars call a "divine passive." In other words, even though the verb "to reckon" is in the passive voice, the readers should understand that God is the agent who does the reckoning. One could render this verse as, "it was reckoned to him *by God* as righteousness." The divine passive intimates that *God's* activity is at the root of justification.

The covenant between God and Abraham (and by extension all Jews) was the consequence of God's gracious initiative. Thus both the Jew and the Jewish Christian would have kept the law not to earn God's favor, but as a faithful response to divine favor already granted. As a Jew, Paul would have realized that the law and faith were not inherently antithetical. Jewish Christians could keep the law as a sign of their faith.[87] For Jews, Abraham's faithful obedience to God's command to be circumcised provided the paradigm of a faithful response to God's grace. Thus it would appear that Paul is arguing not against the law *per se*. Rather, he is arguing against a distorted view of the law that absolutizes Jewish boundary markers, making them the only manifestation of faith and hence the only way to live the covenant relationship.

A Jewish Christian understanding of the manifestation of covenant faith (i.e., keeping the law) is appropriate only insofar as it does not conflict with the very foundation of the covenant. The foundation of the covenant is God's gracious activity, which is appropriated by faith in Jesus Christ, however that faith might manifest itself.

In 3:8 we begin to see Paul's problem with the dominant ideology of the Judaizers more clearly. Paul suggests that inherent in the Judaizers' insistence that Gentiles submit to circumcision is the belief that the covenant promises were meant solely for Jews. Thus if one wanted to inherit the promises, one had to become a Jew. Such a provincial understanding fails to see that in reality the promises were also meant for the Gentiles. James Dunn observes that Paul's argument "is that God's promise always had the Gentiles in view from the beginning."[88]

In this verse Paul writes: "And the scripture, foreseeing that God would justify the Gentiles by faith, proclaimed ahead of time the good news to Abraham: 'All the Gentiles will be blessed in you.'" The covenant, from its very inception, was meant to be universal—one in which *all* the nations would be blessed. This blessing would be bestowed on those of faith. In 3:7 Paul says that people of faith are the children of Abraham (i.e., the covenant people of God). According to 3:8, those who are "in Abraham" will be blessed by God.

Paul's thoughts in 3:7-8 lead him to the conclusion that those from faith will be blessed with Abraham the faithful. Contrary to the dominant ideology—which construed being "in Abraham" as keeping the Jewish law, most notably circumcision—Paul is arguing that in reality what has always constituted being "in Abraham" was living a life from faith. The dominant ideology had a narrow understanding of what being "in Abraham" meant and therefore failed to see the universal intent of the covenant. By enlarging the concept of being "in Abraham," Paul has offered Abraham to the Gentiles as a weapon of resistance to fend off the encroachment of the dominant ideology.

In 3:9 Paul reaches the destination of his excursion. He has shown that from the beginning God had universal aspirations for the covenant and that human participation in the covenant was always intended to be on the basis of faith. According to 3:9, blessings attend covenant membership. In 3:6-9 Paul has instructed his hearers about blessings, so it is logical for him to turn his attention now to what constitutes a curse. Hans Dieter Betz notes: "The logic behind Paul's words, therefore, is simply that exclusion from blessing equals 'curse.'"[89]

In 3:10 Paul identifies the cursed ones as "all who rely on the works of the law" (ὅσοι γὰρ ἐξ ἔργων νόμου). In this case "all who rely on the works of the law" probably refers to *both* the Judaizers who are insisting there is only one way to be a Christian *and* the Gentile converts who are about to adopt the Judaizers' approach. Paul then cites Deut 27:26 as a rationale for this curse.

According to Deut 27:26, a curse arises when one does not remain in all that is written in the book of the law. Since Paul's purpose is to dissuade the Gentile Galatians from adopting a life of law observance he cites a portion of Deuteronomy that highlights a negative aspect of the law. Surely Paul was equally aware of Deutereonomy 28, which presents the blessings God would bestow upon those (Jews) who observed all the Lord's commandments. For the Jew (and ostensibly the Jewish Christian), the law had the potential to bestow a blessing or a curse. Thus in 3:10 Paul does *not* say that those who rely on the law are under a curse. Rather, he says that those who rely on *the works of the law* are under a curse.[90]

In other words, one can draw the conclusion that "to be of the works of the law is not the same as remaining in the law."[91] Jewish Christians could remain in the law as long as they realized that the law was their way to manifest covenant faith, but not the only way. God had made other provisions for the inclusion of the Gentiles, namely a circumcision-free gospel that the Gentiles could accept through faith.

Then, in order that the Galatians might see the utter incompatibility of law-observance and faith *for Gentiles,* Paul in v. 12 declares, "The law is not by faith." Again we must not take Paul's words here as a unilaterally negative assessment of the law.[92] A life of faith and a life of law-observance do not inherently cancel one another out. These two modes of existence, however, are antithetical as far as Gentile believers are concerned. Thus when Paul asserts that the law is not "by faith" he is suggesting that the law causes the Gentiles to focus on the law itself, thereby failing to see that the law is not the end (even for the Jews) but a means to an end. According to Paul, the "price of admission" for all, Jews and Gentiles alike, is faith.

Paul's indignation is not with the law, but with a distorted perspective on the law. He seems to suggest that people who rely on the works of the law[93] are "those who have understood the scope of God's covenant people as Israel per se."[94] In other words, to have a provincial understanding of the scope of God's covenant people is to be under a curse. Such an understanding does not proceed from faith, because faith in Jesus Christ is not a Jewish exclusive. Those from faith are blessed, and according to Paul's logic those who rely on something other than faith are cursed.

Works of the law (or even the law), if they hindered either Jews or Gentiles from seeing the real intent of God's promise, became a curse. Yet the work of Christ has redeemed us from this curse. Commenting on 3:13, James Dunn remarks: "Christ's redemptive work can be specified quite properly as the removal of that curse, as the deliverance of the heirs of the covenant promise from the ill effects of the too narrow understanding of covenant and law held by most of Paul's Jewish contemporaries."[95]

When Paul writes in 3:13 that Christ has redeemed us, both Jews and Gentiles are included in the "us" (ἡμᾶς). The Jewish Christian is released from a provincial understanding of the nature of the law. The Gentile Christian is released from the "necessity" of becoming a Jew and is now free to receive the promises of God as a Gentile. In Christ's death both the "oppressor" and the "oppressed" are liberated. Christ's redemptive work on the cross brings to fruition the original, full-blown design of the covenant. Therefore in 3:14 Paul concludes this section of his argument with the purpose clause, "in order that in Christ Jesus the blessing of Abraham might come to the Gentiles, so that we might receive the promise of the Spirit through faith."

Undoubtedly the proponents of the dominant ideology believed that the covenant was based on faith, but their understanding of faith—manifested in the conviction that one could only be a part of the covenant if one were a Jew—was presumptuous because it overlooked that the Gentiles were also intended to participate in the covenant as *Gentiles.*

As Paul reminds the Gentiles and the Jews that the covenant promises were never meant to be the sole possession of the Jews, so too African Americans, in our quest for liberation, must remind the American power structure that the "promises of America" ought not be the sole possession of white people. Often, as white Americans bask in the light of being natives of the world's largest so-called "democracy," they refer to the Declaration of Independence, which supposedly set forth the promises and principles of the then fledgling nation. When confronted with America's ignoble treatment of African Americans,[96] white Americans occasionally respond that America, in principle if not in practice, is based on the promises offered in the Declaration of Independence. Most cherished of those promises are the inalienable rights of "life, liberty, and the pursuit of happiness."

The African American community hears this response and agrees that in principle these are, or at least ought to be, the promises of America.[97] But the dominant ideology, which has consistently considered African American culture to be substandard, has insisted that African Americans become "white" and adopt white values and lifestyles. Thus the dominant culture has implicitly indicated that it really believes the promises of America to be the sole possession of white Americans; otherwise there would not be such pressure put on African Americans to be like them. Certain white Americans ("Judaizers"), who have a narrow view of the scope of the promises, have told African Americans ("Gentiles") that the rights of life, liberty, and the pursuit of happiness (the "covenant promises of Abraham") really only belong to white people. Thus if we want to enjoy the benefits of these promises we will have to become white (i.e., "we have to judaize"). This understanding of the promises of America is a curse that has prohibited the promises of America from reaching black people.

White society, with impunity, has denied African Americans the right of life. The historical record is full of the gory details of the lynchings and murders of African Americans by whites.[98] In spite of all the violence, very few whites in America have received capital punishment[99] for the murder of a black person. Not only have we been stripped of life and the freedom it affords, but we have also been denied the pursuit of happiness by proponents of the dominant ideology who are under this curse. Disenfranchisement, police brutality, substandard educational resources, inadequate health care, and the lack of political representation have served as shackles on our hands, feet, and minds. When one's hands, feet, and mind are bound, it is hard to pursue happiness.

If African Americans take seriously Paul's words in Gal 3:13-14, then Christ's redemptive work has made it possible for the promises of America to come to "the nations" or "the Gentiles" (τὰ ἔθνη; in this case τὰ ἔθνη is the African American community).[100] In Christ, African Americans have been freed from the curse of the dominant ideology that would force us to become white in order to receive the promises.

But the redemptive work of Christ has also made it possible for white Americans to be freed from a narrow understanding concerning the promises of America. In other words, when African Americans say "yes" to black culture and "no" to white culture, white Americans are compelled to acknowledge the existence of African American culture, even if they are unwilling to appreciate its value. In short, the redemptive work of Christ has redeemed "us," that is, both African Americans and white Americans. Christ's redemptive work liberates both the oppressed and the oppressors.

The curse from which Christ has redeemed African Americans is the curse of being excluded from the promises of America simply by virtue of our blackness. In order for Christ to have become a curse for us, he had to become "black" and experience the suffering that has attended blackness. At the cross Jesus experienced the suffering of being "black," that is, the suffering of being considered an outsider. In the exaltation of Christ in the resurrection God vindicated the "black Jesus" and the concept of blackness. On this point James Cone writes: "Where there is black, there is oppression; but blacks can be assured that where there is blackness, there is Christ who has taken on blackness so that what is evil in men's eyes might become good."[101] The cross has freed us to love and call good that which dominant society has hated and called evil—our blackness.

If African Americans are redeemed in Christ from that curse, then we are free both to be black and to be heirs of all the promises of life in America. Because of the Christ event African Americans must tell dominant society that no longer are the phrases "African American" and "heirs of the American promises" mutually exclusive. Christ has freed us to be unashamedly black!

F. Galatians 3:26-29

> 26. For in Christ Jesus you are all children of God through faith.
> 27. For all of you who have been baptized into Christ have clothed your-selves with Christ.
> 28. There is neither Jew nor Greek, there is neither slave nor free, there is neither male and female; for all of you are one in Christ Jesus.
> 29. And if you belong to Christ, therefore you are the descendants of Abraham, heirs according to the promise.

In the final section of ch. 3 Paul continues to emphasize that faith defines those who have entered into the covenant created by the Christ event. He writes: "For in Christ Jesus you are all children of God through faith." Even though Gentile faith does not involve law observance, Gentiles who accept Christ are in every way God's children. As God's children they have full participation in the blessings of the covenant community.

Paul indicates his concern about the communal implications of a life of faith by the elliptical but important phrase in v. 26 "in Christ Jesus" (ἐν Χριστῷ Ἰησοῦ). The phrase "in Christ Jesus,"[102] which Paul uses frequently in his letters, has received significant attention from scholars.

Many scholars now maintain that the phrase "in Christ Jesus" in Gal 3:26 and elsewhere in Paul's letters is a "formula" connoting the social and ethical implications of communal existence under the lordship of Christ. M. A. Seifrid remarks: "The phrases [in Christ/in the Lord] therefore became a vehicle for Paul to describe the life of faith under Christ's lordship in a world where other powers and temptations were present. To act 'in Christ' is to act in faith and obedience in the face of false alternatives."[103]

The particular "false alternative" against which Paul warns the Galatians is the temptation to submit to law observance. In the Church, the "community of Christ," there are diverse manifestations of faith in Christ, but it is faith in Christ that creates the unity. Thus in v. 26 the words "in Christ Jesus" signify that Paul will discuss the ramifications of being a part of the Church.

In 3:27-28 Paul explores the communal implications of faith in Christ with a liturgical confession used in baptismal services. Many scholars contend that all or part of 3:27-28 was a confession that existed prior to Paul,[104] and that Paul employs and perhaps adapts for his purposes.

Some interpreters have even suggested that this baptismal confession originated as a counter to the three blessings in the Jewish morning prayers: "Blessed be He [God] that did not make me a Gentile; blessed be He that did not make me a boor [i.e., a slave]; blessed be He that did not make me a woman." Possibly, in its original usage and also here in Galatians, this baptismal confession was meant to suggest that "through Christ the old racial schisms and cultural divisions had been healed."[105]

Interestingly, the confession focuses on three spheres that were and are notorious hotbeds of social strife: *ethnic relationships* ("there is neither Jew nor Greek"), *social class* ("there is neither slave nor free"), and *gender relationships* ("there is neither male and female"). Paul is cognizant of the importance of all three spheres in fostering social harmony in the church.[106] In Galatians 3, however, he focuses primarily on the first, namely ethnic relationships. One could argue that the establishment of a proper relationship between Jews and Gentiles who are "in Christ Jesus" is the central challenge that precipitates the writing of the entire letter. I shall limit my discussion to an interpretation of the ethnic implications of Paul's statement in 3:28. Nevertheless, with little difficulty one can apply the insights concerning ethnicity to the spheres of social class and gender relations.

Galatians 3:28 is one of Paul's best-known declarations. Considerable debate and confusion have surrounded its interpretation. In order to achieve an appropriate understanding of this verse we must overturn two misconceptions.

First, some have wrongly assumed that Paul's declaration in v. 28 should be read as an eschatological ideal—a laudable goal that will only be fully accomplished upon the return of Christ. One can question this on rhetorical and grammatical grounds.

This observation does not do justice to the urgency of the "rhetorical situation" in Galatians.[107] Undoubtedly eschatological hope—the assurance that Christ will return and assist in the establishment of God's complete sovereignty—plays an integral role in Paul's overall theology. Paul believed that Christ's return would be imminent.

Yet in the Galatian churches a crisis faced Paul that was even more pressing than Christ's return. With the defection of his converts looming on the horizon it is unlikely that Paul would resort to speculations about the eschatological harmony that Christ would establish. Paul's concern in Galatians 3 is for *present* harmony. From his perspective, without a present remedy to this crisis there very well could be no future for his converts.

Also, grammatically one should note the prevalence of the present tense in v. 28 and, for that matter, in vv. 26-29. Paul declares: "There *is* neither Jew nor Greek, there *is* neither slave nor free, there *is* neither male and female." With the exception of two verbs in the past tense in v. 27, all the verbs in vv. 26-29 are in the present tense. Whatever meaning one gives to v. 28, clearly Paul is conveying a present reality, not a future possibility.

The second misconception is that Christian unity implies or entails the absence of social distinctions. Proponents of this view contend that unity in the Church is achieved through abolishing social distinctions and replacing them with an amalgamated Christian identity. If Paul's declaration in 3:28 was meant to depict the abolishing of social distinctions he would have effectively undercut the force of his whole argument. Paul's entire evangelistic campaign was designed to bring the Gentiles into the Church as Gentiles. In other words, Paul preached a law-free gospel among the Gentiles in order to insure ethnic diversity in the Church. Why, then, would he assert that in Christ the very ethnic diversity for which he had toiled was obliterated in the name of an undifferentiated identity?

When Paul says, "There is neither Jew nor Greek, there is neither slave nor free, there is neither male and female," he is not asserting the obliteration of difference, but rather the obliteration of *dominance*. When one enters the Christian community through belief in Christ and baptism one does not necessarily lose the ethnic, social, or gender distinctions that have characterized one's existence. Even "in Christ" there is still human difference. The dominance of one over the other based on these differences is the reality that is abolished! In Christ, Jews are not to be dominant over Gentiles; free persons are not to be dominant over slaves; men are not to be dominant over women.[108]

Some interpreters have referred to Paul's words in 3:28 as the "Magna Carta" of the New Testament.[109] This declaration affirms that Christ has liberated believers not from the tyranny of difference but from the tyranny of sameness.[110] The particular domination visited upon the Gentiles in Galatia was the coercion for them to be Jews. Quests for unity that presuppose or even demand sameness misconstrue Paul's dynamic, expansive notion of Christian unity.

Our unity in Christ does not consist in an amalgamated or undifferentiated identity. Rather we are "one in Christ" because each Christian individual and each Christian community has a relationship in faith with Christ, and these faith(ful) relationships with Christ are meant to ensure that we relate to each other, in the midst of our many differences, with mutuality and equality. We can only see the truly miraculous nature of Christian unity when the social distinctions that define us are present and even accentuated. An analogy from music may be helpful. Harmony is the cooperative union of different voices. The various vocal parts must maintain their distinctiveness, even as they unite, if harmony is to exist.

Having lifted the shroud of misconception from this important Pauline statement, we can see more clearly how Gal 3:28 can sponsor helpful approaches to equitable race relations in the United States, and more particularly in the Christian church. The deep wounds inflicted by a long history of racism continue to fester. Occasionally the wounds have been covered with the bandage of superficial political rhetoric, but they have rarely received serious attention. In America there is a plethora of races and ethnic groups, and statements of artificial unity that ignore or play down the beauty and complexity of these differences will not resolve the schisms.

As we have argued throughout, unity from an African American standpoint implies the maintenance of cultural distinctions. Misguided and naïve are assertions that America is "the great melting pot" in which distinctive cultural identities are melted into one conglomerate American identity. Heartwarming though this rhetoric may be, the reality behind it has often been a desire to obliterate the identities of non-dominant cultures, thereby making it easier to institutionalize and normalize white American identity.

Utopian visions of a "raceless" American society are the stuff of which "good" campaign speeches are made. Such visions, however, do not provide the foundation for genuine racial unity. If an ideology of a "raceless" society were to emerge after more than three hundred years of white domination it would be tantamount to the maintenance of white domination, but just under a new name. That name would be (artificial) "unity." William Jones remarks: "Annihilation of the race problem by amalgamation is not on the African-American agenda."[111]

Christ has freed the African American to say, "yes" to blackness. Historically, our blackness has been despised. Now under a specious artificial unity being promoted in certain circles our blackness may be ignored. All Americans (and certainly all Christians) should strive for unity, but genuine unity will emerge from a dialogue among culturally distinct groups. Like textual meaning, racial unity is not discovered; it is created or birthed into existence. As with any birth, there is travail. If racial unity is to be brought to life in America, white Americans will have to experience the birth pangs of confronting and dealing with, not ignoring or obliterating the "otherness" of our blackness.

G. Galatians 4:1-11

1. I mean that the heir, as long as he is a minor, is no different from a slave, although he owns all the estate.
2. But he is under guardians and trustees until the appointed time set by the father.
3. So also with us; when we were minors, we were slaves to the elements of the world.
4. But when the fullness of time came, God sent God's son, who was born of a woman and born under the law,
5. in order to redeem those under the law, so that we might receive adoption as children.
6. And because you are children, God sent the Spirit of God's Son in our hearts crying, "Abba! Father!"
7. Therefore, you are no longer a slave but a child, and since a child, then also an heir through God.
8. Formerly, when you did not know God, you were enslaved to beings that by nature are not gods.
9. But now, since you have come to know God, or rather to be known by God, how can you turn again to the weak and beggarly elements? How can you want to be enslaved to them again?
10. You observe days, and months, and seasons, and years.
11. I am afraid that I have labored in vain for you.

Launching the next phase of his argument, Paul employs an illustration from Roman legal practice concerning the guardianship of minors. Many interpretive difficulties surround Paul's use of this illustration. Notwithstanding the difficulties, the plain sense of the illustration is to introduce again the important concept of the inheritance of the covenant promises. Although the minor in this illustration is a rightful heir, while he is under the supervision of the guardians he is no different from a slave in the sense that he is unable to make significant decisions for himself.

Similarly, Paul contends that Jews and Gentiles were in a state of slavery before the Christ event. Paul declares in 4:3: "So also with us; when we were minors, we were slaves to the elements of the world." The interpreter should not underestimate the switch in 4:3 from third person to first person. Paul's words here ("so also with *us*") apply both to Jews and Gentiles. Although both groups were heirs of the covenant promises, bondage under "the elements of the world" prohibited the Jews and Gentiles from enjoying the promises. Who or what are these elements of the world?

There has been extensive scholarly discussion concerning "the elements of the world." A rehearsal of this debate will not detain us here.[112] Yet even without entering that debate we may ascertain Paul's basic meaning. The elements of the world are (demonic) agents who enslave Jews and Gentiles. Only when Jews and Gentiles are redeemed from this slavery can they receive the promises of the covenant. Thus the elements of the world are those beings or forces that prohibit the promises from coming to fruition. Previously Paul cursed anyone or anything that would prohibit the promises from being fulfilled.[113] Thus if the elements of the world attempt to frustrate God's plan Paul likely would consider them accursed or evil. Possibly these accursed elements of the world are responsible for the present age being evil.[114]

In 4:8-10 Paul offers concrete examples of the slavery created by the elements. In 4:8 he identifies idolatry as a manifestation of slavery under the elements. He writes: "Formerly, when you did not know God, you were enslaved to beings that by nature are not gods." Scholars often debate what Paul means by the phrase "beings that by nature are not gods" (τοῖς φύσει μὴ οὖσιν θεοῖς).[115] Irrespective of queries concerning the essence of these "gods," Paul, and the entire biblical tradition, would consider worship of anything except the one true God to be idolatry. Paul earlier (re)defined the children of Abraham as those of faith (in Jesus Christ).[116] Inasmuch as the Gentiles in their idol worship were not expressing a faith in Christ, idol worship was a bondage prohibiting them from enjoying the covenant promises.

In 4:10 we see that certain other practices of Judaism could also be manifestations of slavery under the elements when Gentiles incorporated them. Paul writes: "You observe days, and months, and seasons, and years." Concerning the calendar observances enumerated in this verse, F. F. Bruce notes that possibly "Paul is referring to news which he has just received, to the effect that the Galatians were actually adopting the Jewish calendar."[117] Although there is no formal grammatical connection between Paul's rhetorical question in 4:9 ("How can you turn again to the weak and beggarly elements?") and the mention of the observance of the Jewish calendar in 4:10, commentators generally agree that Paul considers such calendar observances by the Gentiles to be a return to slavery, in the same way as idolatry.

These pernicious elements of the world had enslaved both Jews and Gentiles, but according to 4:4-5 the Christ event has broken the fetters of these elements. In the first clause in v. 5 Paul declares that Christ has redeemed those under the law. "Those under the law"—which could be taken to mean those Jewish Christians who have a distorted perspective on the law—are set free from a narrow viewpoint concerning the scope of the covenant promises. Commentators often suggest that the first clause in 4:5 refers solely to Jewish Christians, yet I surmise that the first clause may also refer to Gentiles as well. Gentiles who wanted to become Christians were also "under the (oppression of the) law" insofar as this narrow perspective on the law remained dominant in early Christianity.

Regardless of my above speculation, Paul includes both Jewish and Gentile Christians in the second clause in 4:5. God sent God's Son "so that *we* might receive adoption as children." By removing the barriers that prohibited Gentiles from entering God's covenant family, Christ's activity is redemptive not only for Gentile Christians, but also for Jewish Christians. The Christ event creates a new family where Jews and Gentiles are on equal footing (Gal 3:28).

Paul indicates the truly revolutionary quality of the Christ event by suggesting that even Jewish Christians are adopted into the new family. Some Jewish Christians might have assumed that as Jews—and thus as the first participants in God's covenant—they were already "children." Paul questions that assumption. To give believers in Christ who are Jewish a preexisting special standing would nullify Paul's claim that Christ had abolished inequality based on ethnicity (and social status, and gender). Commenting on 4:5, Richard Hays remarks: "Paul's adoption metaphor may have another nuance. . . . In contrast to God's own Son, all other human beings, including Jewish believers, enter God's family only by adoption. . . . [The adoption metaphor] must be expanded to include God's adoption of Jewish believers as well."[118]

Christ's liberating activity occurred when the fullness of time came. This phrase ("when the fullness of time came") "belongs to the Jewish and Christian eschatological language which Paul shared,"[119] and can be related to the notion of the fulfillment of time that appears in Paul's illustration in 4:1-2 ("until the appointed time set by the father"). In the illustration, before the fullness of time arrives the child, though in reality an heir, is no better off than a slave. But when the fullness of time comes, the child receives the inheritance.

Applying this illustration in 4:4-7, Paul clearly identifies the Christ event as the indicator that the fullness of time has come. The Christ event makes it possible for Gentiles and Jews to become "children." Lest the Gentiles doubt their status in the family, Paul reminds them that the powerful presence of the Holy Spirit among them confirms unequivocally their adoption and inheritance of the covenant promises.

In 4:7 Paul declares: "Therefore, you are no longer a slave, but a child, and since a child, then also an heir through God." Not only does 4:7 conclude the illustration with which Paul began the chapter, but also it draws together ideas developed in Galatians 3. Throughout Galatians 3–4 Paul has labored persistently to demonstrate to the Galatians that they are children of Abraham and rightful heirs of the promises of the covenant. As a result of the redemptive activity of Christ they are no longer slaves but children and rightful heirs to the covenant blessings.

Galatians 4:1-11 offers crucial insights for the African American liberation movement. Life in twenty-first-century America, for the African American, could very well be considered a "present evil age." All too frequently African Americans are leaders in infamous statistics.

For instance, one could cite the alarming number of homicide felons and victims who are African Americans, as well as the rapid rate at which the HIV/AIDS virus is spreading in the African American community. Additionally, hate crimes toward people of color remain a constant threat. Moreover, on the one hand the powers that be have neglected the urban centers of America, where large numbers of African Americans reside, perhaps with the hope that the "colored problems" in these cities will decay and disintegrate. On the other hand, "urban regentrification" has displaced a significant number of the African American working poor. Recognizing afresh the value of downtown real estate, many architects and contractors are razing urban housing projects and redeveloping these areas as elite residential and commercial districts. Finally, the average income of African Americans continues to fall significantly below that of our white and Asian American counterparts.

I do not know all the reasons why America is a present evil age, but certainly "the elements of the world" (τὰ στοιχεῖα τοῦ κόσμου) have contributed to this reality. As in the ancient case, so too in the modern, "the elements of the world" are beings, forces, and ideologies that would prohibit the promises of America from being disseminated broadly.

In the American context "the elements" assume many forms, yet one may identify racist ideas, which have bolstered the enduring subjugation of African Americans, as a particular manifestation of "the elements." Although the iron shackles that once bound the hands and feet of my forebears have been removed and have long since rusted, ideological shackles have remained around the psyche of African Americans. Thus, nearly 140 years after the end of (chattel) slavery, we still find ourselves in bondage.

African Americans, who are weary of this bondage, are sounding the alarm and bellowing a clarion call: The fullness of time has come! Our ideological liberation draws nigh. For African American Christians the fullness of time may be symbolized in the redemptive work of Christ that emanates to us through the eons of time by the Holy Spirit. For my African American brothers and sisters who are not Christians the fullness of time may be manifest in the spirit of Afrocentric pride that is moving through the land as blacks throw off the yoke of Eurocentric frameworks and (re)discover worldviews more in line with our African ancestors.

Let me digress briefly on this notion of adopting and celebrating ethnically indigenous frameworks and practices. At the ideological level I hope that African American readers take issue with Paul's words in Gal 4:8-9. Speaking to the Gentiles, Paul writes: "Formerly, when you did not know God, you were enslaved to beings that by nature are not gods. But now, since you have come to know God, or rather to be known by God, how can you turn again to the weak and beggarly elements? How can you want to be enslaved to them again?" When these words are read through the lens of African American experience their potentially dangerous implications may emerge clearly.

Throughout Galatians Paul has challenged the dominant ideology, championing the belief that cultural distinctions play a vital role in the fostering of genuine unity. Paul has declared to Gentiles: "Be who you are! You are Gentiles." Paul has encouraged them to acknowledge their heritage as Gentiles, with one exception: they must break from their religious past, which was characterized by idol worship.

Paul's Jewish heritage vividly demonstrates itself in his strong statement against Gentile idolatry. Long before the Christian era Jews incessantly criticized Gentiles for worshiping idols. The Old Testament is replete with exhortations for Jews to avoid the worship of idols because idol worship would associate the Jews with their wayward Gentile neighbors.[120] Many Jews and even Jewish Christians such as Paul assumed that the Gentiles' religious heritage prior to their experience with Christ was illusionary and vacuous.

The Gentiles' religious experience was illusionary because they paid homage to "beings that by nature are not gods" (4:8). Their religious experience was vacuous because in spite of their practices they "did not know God" (4:8). Paul sees no worthwhile connection between the Gentiles' former religious heritage and their current status as Christians.

My point here is not to evaluate the historical or theological validity of the Gentiles' religious heritage before Christ. Rather, I want to demonstrate how the ideological dimensions inherent in Paul's perspective in 4:8-9 have caused an enormous identity crisis among many African American Christians.

Scholars have documented the complex history of white Christian missionary activity in Africa.[121] A major ideological tenet of Christian "missions" to Africa, especially in the eighteenth and nineteenth centuries, was that Africans were ignorant of God prior to the Christian era. Kofi Asare Opoku, a historian of African religion, writes: "In early missionary accounts, the Africans were represented as a people immersed in crippling superstitions, whose religion lacked any abiding values and who were therefore a fitting object of evangelization."[122]

These inaccurate depictions of Africans as "fetishists," "animists," and "idol-worshipers" have caused many African Americans to be ashamed and ignorant of the beautiful, sophisticated religious heritage of Africans prior to the Christian era. Although I, and millions of African Americans, connect with God now through Christianity, Africans knew God long before they had heard of Christianity. I contend that in many regards the African American ignorance of traditional African religions perpetuates, in some sense, our ideological slavery. Rather than exploring the similarities and dissimilarities between traditional African religions and (African American) Christianity, far too many African Americans have jettisoned our African religious history.

I am not advocating the renunciation of our Christian commitments. I believe, however, that the fullness of our theological and ethnic identity as African Americans is not contained solely in our Christian identity. In the ancient biblical context Paul exhorted the Gentiles to sever themselves from their religious past in order to be free. In the contemporary American context the opposite is true. If African Americans continue to sever ourselves from our noble African religious heritage prior to Christianity we create the conditions for our continued ideological slavery.

In "Lift Every Voice and Sing," the Negro National Anthem, James Weldon Johnson prayed that black people would not "stray from the places our God where we met Thee." Too many black people have forgotten that the first place where our ancestors met God was not at the foot of the cross. By opening ourselves to the wisdom and practices of traditional African religions, African American Christians may find much-needed spiritual and psychic resources. These resources may further empower us to drive out "the elements of the world" that bedevil our communities. The African ancestors, so often venerated in traditional African religions, have been waiting to help us. In order to access the ancestors' assistance we need only seek manumission from our slavery to dominant ideology.

The revolutionary bell is ringing. Our servitude to "the elements of the world," in its sundry manifestations, has ended. We are no longer slaves! As we seek freedom in all its facets this phrase should be the manifesto of our emancipatory quest: "We are no longer slaves!"

H. Galatians 5:13-26

13. For you were called to freedom, brothers and sisters; only do not let the freedom become an opportunity for the flesh, but through love become slaves to one another.

14. For all the law is fulfilled in one commandment: "Love your neighbor as yourself."

15. But if you bite and devour one another, watch out lest you be consumed by one another.

16. This is what I mean: walk by the Spirit and you will not at all[123] perform the desires of the flesh.

17. For the flesh desires against the Spirit. The Spirit desires against the flesh. These entities[124] are opposed to each other, so that you do not do what you want.

18. But if you are led by the Spirit, you are not under the law.

19. And the works of the flesh are clear: These are fornication, impurity, indecency,

20. idolatry, sorcery, hostility, strife, jealousy, anger, selfishness, dissension, factions,

21. envy, drunkenness, carousing, and other things like these. I warn you, as I warned you before, that those who practice such things will not inherit the kingdom of God.

22. But the fruit of the spirit is love, joy, peace, patience, kindness, goodness, faithfulness,

23. meekness, and self-control. Against such things there is no law.

24. And those who belong to Christ have crucified the flesh with its passions and desires.

25. If we live by the Spirit, let us also walk by the Spirit.

26. Let us not become conceited, nor provoke one another, nor become envious of one another.

In 5:13 Paul reminds the Galatians of their call to freedom. Lest, however, this call to freedom be misunderstood or misappropriated, Paul offers moral instructions. In the history of Pauline scholarship some have considered the ethical exhortations in Paul's letters to be "filler" with no integral relationship to his theology. Victor Furnish remonstrates against such a view. He writes: "The apostle's ethical concerns are not secondary but radically integral to his basic theological convictions."[125]

The connection between theology and ethics is so close that John Barclay suggests that the threat of the Gentiles submitting to the law was in reality a result of Paul's theology. According to Barclay's very plausible historical reconstruction, the Galatians heard and responded favorably to the gospel proclaimed by Paul. Their acceptance of the gospel, however, was not without cost. Barclay observes:

> As Christian converts they [the Galatians] had abandoned the worship of pagan deities (4:8-11) and this conversion would have involved not only massive cognitive readjustments but also social dislocation. To disassociate oneself from the worship of family and community deities would entail a serious disruption in one's relationships with family, friends. . . . Paul's presence in Galatia and his creation of Christian communities there had helped to establish a social identity for these Christians. . . . his departure from Galatia must have underlined their social insecurity.[126]

Having accepted Paul's message of freedom and become Christians, the Galatians found themselves dealing with the anxiety that often accompanies an ambiguous and precarious social identity. Also, possibly, their anxiety stemmed from an ignorance concerning the rules that should regulate their lives. By judaizing, the Gentiles "could hope to identify themselves with the local synagogues and thus hold a more understandable and recognizable place in society."[127] In obedience to Torah they could find information and structure for daily living.

The benefits of judaizing were attractive, but Paul warned the Galatians against the wooing ways of the judaizers,[128] lest the Galatians be seduced and find themselves again under the yoke of slavery. In short, it is historically plausible that Paul's preaching of freedom paradoxically may have driven the Galatians to that yoke.

Therefore Paul explains or qualifies his notion of freedom and in so doing sets up his own paradox. This freedom that he preached was not unbridled. To the contrary, this freedom was actually manifested in "slavery"—a slavery to the welfare of one's neighbors (5:13).[129] John Barclay notes: "This paradox shows that the freedom he advocates has stringent moral obligations built into it—not the obligation of the law but the obligation of love."[130] Then, in 5:14, Paul contends that the whole law is fulfilled in the command to love the neighbor. This verse has perplexed interpreters because Paul seems to be saying rather positive things about the law, and elsewhere he has said supposedly negative things about the law. Briefly, can we make sense of this problem?

The difficulty of this verse might dissipate if we remember that Paul is not categorically opposed to the law; rather, he criticizes an improper understanding of the law. Previously Paul has taken ideas that were present in the debate between himself and the Judaizers and used them creatively as support for his position.[131] Perhaps a similar phenomenon is operative here.

The law seemed to have been attractive to the Galatians. Thus Paul tells them that if they love their neighbor they have in reality satisfied the whole law, that is, "the basic commandments that contain and sum up the whole law."[132] Consequently there is no need for the Galatians to submit to the law. While avoiding the appearance of promoting the law,[133] Paul impresses upon the Galatians that love for the neighbor fulfills the real intent of the law and does not threaten their freedom in Christ.[134]

If the law is not the safeguard against sin and the misuse of freedom, what is? Paul would respond resolutely, "The Holy Spirit!" Thus in 5:16 he writes: "This is what I mean: walk by the Spirit, and you will not at all perform the desires of the flesh." The importance of the experience of the Spirit has run throughout the letter[135] and receives expression once again. The same Spirit that created and confirmed the Galatians' covenant acceptance by God is also sufficient to guide their moral affairs.

Having instructed the Galatians about the efficacy of the Spirit as a moral guide, Paul offers a list of behaviors that are characteristic of life under the flesh; these he calls "the works of the flesh." Then he offers a list of virtues that are characteristic of a life led by the Spirit; these he calls "the fruit of the Spirit."

Many commentators have attempted to categorize these vices and virtues. Such classifications may be helpful, but what is of importance for an African American hermeneutic is that a large majority of both the vices and virtues have to do with behaviors that either destroy or edify the community. A general characteristic of the works of the flesh is that they destroy unity and community. A general characteristic of the fruit of the Spirit is that they promote corporate well-being. Interpreters should not overlook the social aspects of Paul's ethical admonitions. The Spirit empowers believers to seek what is right not only in their relationships with God but also in their relationships with other people.

Like Paul, I dare not end my manifesto concerning African American freedom without some word for my brothers and sisters about ethics. Our liberation will come neither easily nor quickly. Thus as we struggle incessantly for ideological and socio-political freedom, ethical guidelines to govern our behavior are necessary and helpful. We need moral guidelines that will empower us to deal with "sin" or what Paul here calls "the works of the flesh." Moreover, we need ethics that will prohibit us from misusing our freedom.

Before discussing some of the ethical insights that must buttress our liberation efforts I shall digress briefly to discuss the meaning of sin in the African American context. In Chapter One we saw that Eugene Genovese suggested that Africa bequeathed to her progeny a different understanding of sin than Europe bequeathed to hers. Therefore African Americans have historically given a different nuance to their understanding of sin. The emphasis on social realities, so frequently discussed in this book, also applies to the African American understanding of sin.

Sin is a social reality and not just a personal reality.[136] It is telling that Paul refers to the forces that destroy community in the plural: "the works of the flesh" and "the elements of the world." The forces that oppose freedom are not singular, nor do they wage war simply on the personal level. They are collective forces that attack whole cultures. William Jones poignantly expresses the social nature of sin from an African American standpoint. He writes:

> When sin becomes structured and inequity is institutionalized, the resultant arrangement is ineluctably wicked and nefarious, for it denies other human beings access to the tree of life. This is the continuing tragedy of

America. The victims are correct when they speak of the nation in terms of "The System" for they correctly address themselves to that power arrangement in society based on wealth and whiteness, which prevents the gap between the needy and the greedy from closing. The System is racist to the very core. So deep and so pervasive is the reality that its bitter fruits multiply even without cultivation.[137]

To counteract sin along with its bitter fruit, African Americans must cultivate the fruit of the Spirit. Paul's reference to the virtues that edify community as "fruit" may be no accident. Commenting on the phrase "fruit of the Spirit," Richard Longenecker suggests that Paul is not implying in this phrase an "ethical passivity."[138] The appropriate ethics for African American liberation will not merely be placed in us by the Spirit. Rather, with the aid of the Spirit we must help this fruit to blossom. In order to confront the collectivized negativity of "the works of the flesh" and "the elements of the world" heroic effort, inspired by the Spirit, will be required on our part. Our chance to eat from the American tree of life or share in the American promises may rest on our ability to foster behaviors that promote communal as well as personal fulfillment.

In a way very similar to Paul's ethics, in the ethics that will sustain the African American liberation movement the Spirit will play a significant role. The experiences of African American slaves have provided an important touchstone in this book. The slave narratives, which only of late have been admitted into the canon of historically valid documents,[139] offer interesting insights into what the Spirit's role has been in African American tradition.

For African American slaves the Spirit was the force that helped them maintain their dignity even in the face of the psychic indignities heaped upon them daily by the dehumanizing institution of slavery. Commenting on the slaves' understanding of the Spirit, George Cummings writes: "The Spirit's presence . . . entailed the affirmation of independence and selfhood; sustained hope for freedom as embodied in their prayer life; served as the basis of love within the slave community; and even assisted slaves in their desire to escape to freedom."[140]

African Americans have envisioned the Spirit as a power that operates not only in the personal realm but also in the social realm. The Spirit in ancient Galatia may have evoked the cry, "Abba! Father!" (Gal 4:6). But in contemporary America the Spirit is birthing within African Americans a mentality of defiance with respect to "the elements of the world." Empowered by the Spirit, we can protest against and defy all those forces and beings that would strip away our dignity and freedom.

In Paul's ethics the Spirit plays a decided social role; the Spirit is concerned about the welfare of the community. The Spirit likewise plays a large social role in African American experience. The borders defining the community in which the Spirit is operative, however, differ slightly for Paul and for African Americans. For Paul one may suppose that the work of the Spirit is a decidedly "ecclesial" phenomenon. In other words, the Spirit is active primarily, if not exclusively, among Christians who constitute the *ekklēsia* or the Church. Paul's ethics are religious ethics meant to regulate the Christians' dealings, especially with other Christians but also with non-Christians.

The Spirit, which empowers believers to behave in prescribed ways, is activated through faith in Christ. Paul urges the Galatians to exemplify good conduct toward all people. Yet even within that universal concern Paul shows a particular care for those who are members of the Christian community. In 6:10 he writes: "So, therefore, as we have opportunity, let us do good to all people, and especially to those who are of the household of faith."

From an African American perspective the work of the Spirit can also be understood as a religious phenomenon, but the Spirit's activity should not be construed as being exclusively tied to the Church. African Americans cannot afford to be circumscribed by an overly narrow conception of the parameters of the Spirit's ministry. In the conclusion of Chapter Two I discussed the dialogue between Jesus and Nicodemus in John 3. During that interchange Jesus acknowledges the "transgressive" character of the Spirit, that is, the Spirit's mysterious habit of crossing or even disregarding our restrictive boundaries. Jesus tells Nicodemus: "The wind blows wherever it wills." When speaking of the wind Jesus uses the same word that is used to describe the Holy Spirit, *pneuma* (πνεῦμα). Thus Jesus implies that since the Spirit is like the wind, no one can predict or prohibit the Spirit's free movement. So also African American Christians should not presume that the Spirit's ministry is restricted simply to the Church.

In the name of freedom we must affirm that the Spirit is operative not only among those who believe Jesus Christ is Lord, but also among those African Americans who seek to defy "the elements of the world." Wherever the curses of racism and other forms of subjugation are found, there, too, the Spirit can be found trying to redeem oppressed people from those curses. Both inside and outside of the African American Church or "household of faith," the Spirit is at work.

In the black Church the religious is social, and the social is religious, perhaps to a much greater degree than in the white Church. Thus there have been significant links between the Christian and non-Christian segments of the African American community, especially with respect to the struggle against racism. A passage from the Gospel of Mark illustrates this.

In Mark 9:38-41 an exorcist casts out demons. Jesus' disciples rebuke the exorcist because he was not a follower of Jesus. Jesus, however, responds to the disciples, "Do not hinder him . . . for whoever is not against us is for us."[141]

From an African American vantage point I interpret Jesus' words to mean that when people are engaging in the serious work of exorcising the "demonic" spirits of racism and other forces that nullify human wholeness there is little time to quibble over religious, denominational, or doctrinal differences. In our struggle for freedom African American Christians must join forces with other African Americans, regardless of religious persuasion or the lack thereof. Even though many African Americans are not followers in the Christian way, inasmuch as they may be casting out demons in their own spheres of influence, places of employment, organizations, and communities, they are for us.

As we press for our liberation, our ethical guideline must be love for all neighbors, but we are to do good especially to those of the household of African Americans. Paul's appeal to the love commandment is extremely timely for African Americans because there is a spirit of hate and self-destruction—generated maybe in response to "the elements of the world"—that is decimating the African American community. This wicked spirit especially manifests itself in black-on-black violence and the rise of suicide among African Americans.

Duped by "the elements of the world" into believing that their black lives are worthless and overwhelmed by the despair of hopelessness, many African American youth have resorted to fatalistic violence against one another. Such violence, in which we are biting, devouring, and consuming ourselves, is antithetical to liberation (Gal 5:15). The Spirit empowering our struggle inspires creative defiance, not communal destruction. African Americans have traditionally lived by the power of this creative and defiant Spirit. If we are to be free, in our journey towards liberation we must continue to walk by that Spirit.

Even before African people were introduced to Christianity they knew intimately the Spirit about whom Paul speaks. That Spirit was present in the beat of the African drum and in the ecstasy of the African dance. That Spirit was in the minds of Africans as they developed the blueprint of world civilization and created culture, religion, science, medicine, architecture, and commerce. That Spirit sustained African exiles in the stinking hulls of slave ships. When the master took away the slaves' shoes to keep them from running, that Spirit told the slaves that in heaven "all God's children got shoes."[142]

Moreover, many African Americans know intuitively that this same Spirit is in the gospel songs we intone, the blues we moan, the jazz we be-bop, and the rap music we hip-hop. This same Spirit, which has given us hopeful "music" in the darkest of our midnights, is supremely able to instill in us behaviors that will result in our communal freedom. Since African people for millennia have lived by this Spirit, let twenty-first-century African Americans walk by this Spirit!

CONCLUSION

Regardless of one's appraisal of these interpretations, this book has attempted to bear the reality it proclaims. I have called for an ideological emancipation from the dominant ideology to correspond to the physical emancipation from slavery that African Americans experienced nearly 140 years ago. Thus I have endeavored to offer critical, faithful readings of both experience and Scripture that depart from the dominant paradigms that have governed so much New Testament interpretation and theology. The African American ideological exodus in the twenty-first century may be no less lengthy and arduous than our transition in the nineteenth century from physical slavery to freedom. An African American hermeneutic is, perhaps, a substantive step along liberation's highway.

I trust that this book makes at least two perceptible, though modest, contributions. First, it may serve as an example of African American critical thought. Cornel West suggests that this critical thought "is a genre of writing, a textuality, a mode of discourse that interprets, describes, and evaluates Afro-American life in order comprehensively to understand and effectively to transform it."[143] In order to produce African American critical thought I had to recognize that the way a book is written is as important as the ideas contained therein. In one sense, the medium is the message.

For example, the structure of the book is very telling. Though there is serious, critical engagement with Scripture (Chapter Three) and with interpretive methodology (Chapter Two), our liberation may first depend on a critical assessment of African American experience. Thus an accounting of salient aspects of that experience (Chapter One) provided the rubric for the reading of Scripture and the use of interpretive methodology. Even in the crucial work of biblical interpretation African Americans cannot simply go straight to the Bible. Biblical interpretation without interpretation of the African American experience provides no basis to understand or transform African American life.

With respect to textual interpretation, African American critical thought is a mode of discourse that negates an essentialist approach to textual meaning. There is no pre-existent, essential meaning of Galatians (or any text) for African Americans that can be discovered apart from the experience of African Americans. The experience is not some shell that can be thrown away once the meaning of the text is discovered. The experience is constitutive of the meaning.

Second, this book may contribute to New Testament theology by emphasizing the communal context in which theology occurs. The New Testament documents themselves provide substantive evidence that "God-talk" occurs in community and must be related to the present life of the community in question. Contemporary African Americans, like ancient Christians, want to make sense of God-talk, yet we recognize that the God of whom we speak and from whom we intend to hear cannot be known apart from description.

Stephen Moore remarks: "Description can proceed only from within some comprehensive context or situation (socio-economic, cultural, gender-specific, institutional, etc.) that yields up the object of description."[144] By highlighting African American history and culture as the context (and perhaps pretext) for my emancipatory theology, I acknowledge the culturally conditioned nature of theology and openly admit my cultural position in order to proceed with the business of description and interpretation.

Advocates of liberationist perspectives have routinely criticized dominant theological paradigms on two fronts. Dominant paradigms have often remained either abstract or myopic. In the first instance dominant theological musings have often refused to engage real life and its messy, yet magnificent manifestations. In the second instance, on those occasions when dominant theological articulations have intersected real life they have assumed that by addressing white experience they have commented on all experience. By emphasizing the African American *community* I have sought to rectify the preoccupation with abstraction. By emphasizing the *African American* community I have sought to enlarge the Church's and the academy's scope of vision.

In spite of my assessment, ultimately others will and must judge the quality of this act of "intellectual abolition." Nevertheless, I pray that God and the ancestors will be pleased with my efforts.

Nearly two thousand years ago Paul told a group of Christian converts that they were no longer slaves. As history would have it, another group of people, children of the African Diaspora resident on American soil, would encounter Paul's declaration of independence and earnestly attempt to decipher his words in light of their physical and ideological slave experience. Because of our slave experience African Americans may view Paul's words as more than simple historical relics to be discussed dispassionately in scholarly commentaries. Read through the lens of our experience, these words may be a defiant declaration to pursue resolutely our God-given freedom.

In Gal 4:7 Paul says: "Therefore you are no longer a slave but a child, and since a child, then also an heir through God." I have offered plausible readings of what this New Testament passage and the epistle in which it is found may mean to contemporary African Americans. However, the unswerving commitment to freedom that African Americans may see in Paul's words is best captured in the language of my ancestors who both lived through slavery and believed that God desired humanity to be free.

> O Freedom! O Freedom!
> O Freedom over me!
> An' before I'd be a slave,
> I'll be buried in my grave,
> An' go home to my Lord
> an' be free.[145]

If it costs us our lives, we are determined to be slaves no longer!

NOTES: CHAPTER 3

[1] This chapter offers an indicative and not exhaustive treatment of Galatians. In order to honor my goal of providing an accessible yet critical introduction to a liberating African American hermeneutic I needed to exercise some selectivity.

[2] The call is the experience whereby Paul became a follower of Christ. Scholars sometimes refer to this event as a "call" rather than a "conversion" because the term "conversion" may inaccurately connote that Paul changed religions. By exercising faith in Christ, Paul did not adopt a new religion *per se.* As a follower of Christ, Paul may have abandoned (certain tenets of) Pharisaic Judaism, but not Judaism altogether. Daniel Boyarin remarks: "Paul lived and died convinced that he was a Jew living out Judaism. He represents, then, one option which Judaism could take in the first century." *A Radical Jew: Paul and the Politics of Identity* (Berkeley: University of California Press, 1994) 2. John M. G. Barclay also interprets Paul's apostolic activity as a critique and development of Jewish tradition and not so much a departure from it. See Barclay's very insightful discussion of Paul's anomalous Jewish identity in his *Jews in the Mediterranean Diaspora: From Alexander to Trajan (323 B.C.E.–117 C.E.)* (Edinburgh: T & T Clark, 1996) 381–95. Also see John Gager's critique of the debate about referring to Paul's experience as a "conversion" or a "call" in his *The Origins of Anti-Semitism: Attitudes Toward Judaism in Pagan and Christian Antiquity* (New York: Oxford University Press, 1983) 209–10.

[3] Loveday Alexander, "Chronology of Paul," in Gerald F. Hawthorne, Ralph P. Martin, and Daniel G. Reid, eds., *Dictionary of Paul and His Letters* (Downers Grove, Ill.: Intervarsity Press, 1993) 117. For another standard treatment of the complicated issues of Pauline chronology see Robert Jewett, *A Chronology of Paul's Life* (Philadelphia: Fortress, 1979). For a helpful comparison of some leading scholarly reconstructions of Paul's chronology see Calvin J. Roetzel, *Paul: The Man and the Myth* (Columbia, S.C.: University of South Carolina Press, 1998) 178–83.

[4] C.E. is a scholarly abbreviation for "Common Era." It is interchangeable with the abbreviation "A.D." Scholars most often use 30 or 33 C.E. as the date of Jesus' crucifixion; the call of Paul (34 C.E.), therefore, is chronologically very close to the ministry of Jesus.

[5] Scholars also refer to this as the first Macedonian journey.

[6] See C. K. Barrett, *Freedom & Obligation: A Study of the Epistle to the Galatians* (Philadelphia: Westminster, 1985) 3–4.

[7] As we shall see, the Galatian converts were marginalized in the sense that certain Jewish Christian preachers may have informed them that their experience with the Holy Spirit was not sufficient to completely bring them into the

Christian family. In order to be fully accepted, the Galatians were being persuaded to submit to circumcision, thereby becoming ethnic Jews.

[8] All translations of the Greek text in this chapter are mine.

[9] Literally the Greek does not have "and sisters." Like other modern translators, I have inserted this for gender inclusiveness.

[10] See J. Louis Martyn's insightful comments on Paul's understanding of the gospel as an apocalyptic *event* that supplants and transforms previous religious tradition. *Galatians* (New York: Doubleday, 1997) 149.

[11] Gal 1:16.

[12] J. Louis Martyn remarks: "Paul's rhetoric presupposes God's action through Paul's words." Thus even in his letter writing Paul is proclaiming the gospel. *Galatians* 23.

[13] Paul cryptically refers to this experience in Gal 1:15-16; see also 1 Cor 15:8-11.

[14] For a highly accessible discussion of the christological questions that engaged the Church in the second through the fifth centuries of the Common Era see Boniface Ramsey, *Beginning to Read the Fathers* (New York: Paulist, 1985) 72–94.

[15] *A Greek-English Lexicon of the New Testament and Other Early Christian Literature (BAGD)*, edited by Frederick William Danker. Third Edition. Based on Walter Bauer's *Griechisch-deutsches Wörterbuch zu den Schriften des Neuen Testaments und der frühchristlichen Literatur,* Sixth Edition (Chicago and London: University of Chicago Press, 2000) 1079.

[16] Francis Brown, S. R. Driver, and Charles A. Briggs, *A Hebrew and English Lexicon of the Old Testament* (Oxford: Clarendon Press, 1951) 1022–23.

[17] For further insight on Paul's christology in Galatians see Richard Hays, "Christology and Ethics in Galatians: The Law of Christ," *Catholic Biblical Quarterly* 49 (1987) 268–90.

[18] The English phrase "in order that" is a translation of one Greek word, ὅπως. In Greek grammar the use of this word as a conjunction would have alerted listeners that the succeeding words indicated the *purpose* of the intended or completed action.

[19] The Greek verb Paul uses in 1:6 has the connotation of exasperation.

[20] Bauer, *A Greek-English Lexicon* 513.

[21] During the last two centuries much African American literature has been an attempt to impart to black people that they have an authenticity that supercedes any (dis)approval of white people. For example, see the fiction of Zora Neale Hurston and the poetry of Langston Hughes.

[22] In Galatians, Paul alludes to "the elements of the world" (τὰ στοιχεῖα), which may be large forces outside the world that seek to impinge on and negatively affect the course of human events. There may be many contemporary analogues for the "elements of the world," and I believe that white supremacy may be as good an analogue as any. See my interpretation of Gal 4:1-11 below. For a useful historical overview of white supremacy in America see Stephan Thernstrom and Abigail Thernstrom, *America in Black and White: One Nation, Indivisible* (New York: Simon & Schuster, 1997) 25–52. Also for a recent treatment of the enduring reality of white racism in America see Joe R. Feagin, "Fighting White Racism: The Future of Equal Rights in the United States," in Samuel L. Myers, Jr., ed., *Civil Rights and Race Relations in the Post-Reagan-Bush Era* (Westport, Conn.: Praeger, 1997) 29–45.

[23] Carlyle Fielding Stewart, *Soul Survivors: An African American Spirituality* (Louisville: Westminster John Knox, 1997) 43–44.

[24] William H. Myers, "The Hermeneutical Dilemma of the African American Biblical Student," in Cain Hope Felder, ed., *Stony the Road We Trod: African American Biblical Interpretation* (Minneapolis: Fortress, 1991) 55.

[25] Frederick Douglass, "The Significance of Emancipation in the West Indies," August 3, 1857, in John W. Blassingame, ed., *The Frederick Douglass Papers*, Series One (New Haven: Yale University Press, 1985) 3:204.

[26] The black feminist bell hooks has issued a challenge for black thinkers (at the grassroots and in academic institutions) to reclaim our ability to analyze *critically* the work that black people produce, and not just accept it blindly because it is done by black people. hooks writes, "The notion that cultural criticism by black folks must either be confined to the question of positive or negative representation or function in a self-serving manner (that is, if you are talking about a work by a black person then you must say something positive or risk being 'silenced') must be continually challenged." *Yearning: race, gender, and cultural politics* (Boston: South End Press, 1990) 7.

[27] Though this phrase is not in the Greek, I have inserted it for the sake of clarity.

[28] Interestingly, even though the three accounts of Paul's call in Acts vary in detail, they agree that Paul did go into Damascus after his encounter with Jesus. See Acts 9:19, 22:11, and 26:20.

[29] Gal 1:13-14.

[30] Hans Dieter Betz, *Galatians* (Philadelphia: Fortress, 1979) 76.

[31] Paul probably refers to Peter, James, and John as "pillars" (στῦλοι) in order to underscore their foundational role in the leadership of the early Christian movement.

[32] The Greek verb Paul uses to describe these leaders (δοκέω) carries the connotations of appearing, supposing, imagining, or having a subjective opin-

ion. In other words, in their own eyes these Jerusalem leaders may have considered themselves persons of significant influence and authority, but in Paul's opinion their influence and authority were no greater than his as an apostle commissioned by Christ.

[33] Carter G. Woodson, *The Mis-Education of the Negro* (Washington, D.C.: Associated Publishers, 1933; reprint Trenton, N.J.: African World Press, 2000) 134.

[34] George Howard, *Paul: Crisis in Galatia: A Study in Early Christian Theology* (Cambridge: Cambridge University Press, 1979) 40.

[35] In an important recent study of Paul's approach to ethnicity (*A Radical Jew: Paul and the Politics of Identity* [Berkeley: University of California Press, 1994]), Daniel Boyarin contends that one of Paul's impulses was to found "a non-differentiated, non-hierachical humanity," and this impulse required "that all human cultural specificities—first and foremost, that of the Jews—be eradicated" (8). It would stand to reason that if this were Paul's impulse (I am doubtful that it was, and even if this impulse did exist, it was by no means dominant), his aims would have been better served by preaching a gospel of circumcision among the Gentiles rather than preaching a circumcision-free gospel. If he had preached a gospel of circumcision he would have created the kind of homogenization that Boyarin says Paul sought. On the contrary, by preaching a circumcision-free gospel among the Gentiles as he actually did, Paul was working against those who wanted Christianity to be ethnically monolithic. Boyarin's theory that Paul desired a univocal humanity is derived by placing too much emphasis on Gal 3:26-28 and by giving an undue amount of weight to the (relatively minor) role of allegory in Paul's interpretive scheme. Even though Galatians does show some universal concern (e.g., Paul's mention of the present evil age in 1:4 and his exhortation to do good *to all* in 6:10), Paul's principal concern in Galatians is not *humanity* as such. His interest is to define what the appropriate contours of the church (ἐκκλεσία) should be in light of God's work in Christ. Galatians is primarily a Pauline critique of the Church from the inside and not a manifesto for the creation of a "univocal humanity." The question is not whether Paul wanted to erase all human differences unilaterally. Instead, the questions for Paul are: when is the affirmation of human difference appropriate, and when does the affirmation of difference obscure Christ's work to create an end-time community that unites even across differences? Perhaps Paul's conflict is not with cultural distinctives on the whole but with the superimposition of those distinctives on other believers as if those distinctives were the only norm. Paul's evangelistic campaign among the Gentiles suggests that ethnic distinctives certainly have their place, but when these distinctives become the very basis of dissolution within the Church they must be re-examined and possibly relativized.

[36] Betz, *Galatians* 82.

[37] I say "natural" in the sense that the "kingdom of God movement" that Jesus inherited from John the Baptist and then amplified in his own way was primarily a Jewish affair. Although the Gospels indicate that Jesus regularly and willingly came into contact with Gentiles (e.g., Matt 8:5-13 and Mark 7:24-30), they also suggest that Jesus understood his mission to be principally among fellow Jews (e.g., Matt 10:5-15). Additionally, the religion about Jesus that sprung up after his death and resurrection also began exclusively as a Jewish phenomenon. In fact, according to Acts 11:19-30, Christianity may have become a named entity distinguishable from a kind of messianic Judaism precisely because the missionaries in Antioch purposefully attempted to bring Gentiles into the church with Jews. Jesus' own religion was Judaism, and even the religion about Jesus in its beginnings was a form of Judaism. Thus it would stand to reason that those who wanted to participate in this religion about Jesus would need to become Jews.

[38] This is the name often given to the group of conservative Jewish Christians who believed that Gentiles must first become Jews in order to enter the church. For further discussion see William S. Campbell, "Judaizers," in Gerald F. Hawthorne, Ralph P. Martin, and Daniel G. Reid, eds., *Dictionary of Paul and His Letters* (Downers Grove, Ill.: Intervarsity Press, 1993) 512–16.

[39] Howard, *Paul: Crisis in Galatia* 79.

[40] For more information on the history of Antioch see LaMoine F. Devries, "Antioch," *Cities of the Biblical World* (Peabody, Mass.: Hendrickson, 1998) 345–50. Also see Raymond E. Brown and John P. Meier, *Antioch and Rome: New Testament Cradles of Catholic Christianity* (New York: Paulist, 1983) 12–84.

[41] In 2:12 Paul uses the imperfect tense of the verb "to eat with" (συνήσθειν). In Greek the imperfect tense is often employed to depict habitual action. Thus Paul may be implying that Peter ate with the Gentiles on a repeated, even regular basis.

[42] Paul uses the imperfect tense of the verbs "to withdraw" (ὑπέστελλεν) and "to separate" (ἀφώριζεν), which again possibly connotes that once the representatives from James came, Peter made it his regular practice to separate from the Gentiles.

[43] Betz, *Galatians* 108.

[44] Ibid. 108.

[45] James D. G. Dunn, "The Theology of Galatians: The Issue of Covenantal Nomism," in Jouette M. Basler, ed., *Pauline Theology: Thessalonians, Philippians, Galatians, Philemon* (Minneapolis: Fortress, 1991) 139.

[46] Diaspora is the term used to describe Jewish communities that existed outside the land of Israel.

[47] In no way do I mean to imply that the reconceptualizations of the religious and cultural valences of circumcision and uncircumcision among both

ancient Jewish and Gentile Christians would have been an easy (or at times desirable) process by either camp. Modern interpreters are often too far removed from the enormous *symbolic* significance that being circumcised or uncircumcised would have had in the ancient world. By symbolic significance I mean that the act of being circumcised or remaining uncircumcised invited and presupposed participation in larger systems of meaning. From the Jewish perspective circumcision would have made one a "man of the covenant." Additionally, from a certain symbolic perspective of the Jewish covenant Gentiles who remained uncircumcised submitted themselves to the risk, or more pointedly, the inevitability of future destruction (e.g., Ps 2:8-9; Mic 5:15). From the Gentile symbolic perspective submission to circumcision would have been considered bodily mutilation and an indication of Jewish misanthropy. Rather than viewing circumcision as a commitment to community, Gentiles would have interpreted this "strange rite" as a sign of the Jewish desire for seclusion from the larger Greco-Roman world. For example, in his *Histories* the Roman historian Tacitus remarks: "Whatever their origin, these [Jewish] rites are maintained by their antiquity: the other customs of the Jews are base and abominable. . . . [T]he Jews are extremely loyal toward one another . . . but toward every other people they feel only hate. . . . [T]hey adopted circumcision to distinguish themselves from other peoples by this difference. . . ." Quoted from Lawrence H. Schiffman, *Texts and Traditions: A Source Reader for the Study of Second Temple and Rabbinic Judaism* (Hoboken, N.J.: Ktav Publishing House, 1998) 200. Consequently the attempt of Jewish or Gentile Christians in Pauline churches to affirm their difference through either circumcision or uncircumcision, without attaching to such affirmations the usual associations noted above, would have required considerable effort. For further discussion of the significance of circumcision and uncircumcision in Pauline churches see Brad Ronnell Braxton, *The Tyranny of Resolution: I Corinthians 7:17-24* (Atlanta: Society of Biblical Literature, 2000) 129–76.

[48] Lester L. Grabbe, *Leviticus* (Sheffield: Sheffield Academic Press, 1993) 59.

[49] Whether written by Paul or one of Paul's disciples, Eph 2:14 captures the notion that the stereotypes that prohibited fellowship between Jews and Gentiles had been overcome in Christ. "He [Christ] is our peace, having made the two [i.e., Jews and Gentiles] one and having destroyed the dividing wall of hatred in his flesh . . ." Ethnic stereotypes among Jews and Gentiles may have helped to erect this "dividing wall of hatred" that Christ came to dismantle.

[50] The etymological roots of the word "hypocrite" (ὑποκριτής) extend to Greek drama. The word denoted an actor or one who put on a mask in order to assume a role in a play. From this meaning come the connotations of deception and duplicity.

[51] The verb "to withdraw" (ὑποστέλλω) carried the connotation of a political or military retreat to a safe position. See Betz, *Galatians* 108.

[52] In the Greek the personal pronoun "you" is strongly emphasized.

[53] See my discussion of Nicodemus in Chapter Two.

[54] James D. G. Dunn, *Jesus, Paul, and the Law: Studies in Mark and Galatians* (London: S.P.C.K., 1990) 189.

[55] Howard, *Paul: Crisis in Galatia* 46.

[56] Krister Stendahl, *Paul Among Jews and Gentiles* (Philadelphia: Fortress, 1977).

[57] E. P. Sanders, *Paul and Palestinian Judaism: A Comparison of Patterns of Religion* (London: S.C.M. Press, 1977).

[58] Dunn, *Jesus, Paul, and the Law* 219.

[59] In the Greek one sees more naturally the fourfold division of the clauses.

[60] In 2:16 Paul uses a participial form of the verb "to know," in the perfect tense, which could connote that the conviction he is about to espouse has been true in the past and continues to be true even in the present.

[61] Sanders, *Paul and Palestinian Judaism* 180 (emphasis in the original).

[62] Dunn, *Jesus, Paul, and the Law* 191.

[63] Ibid. 192.

[64] Ibid. 193.

[65] Sanders, *Paul and Palestinian Judaism* 205.

[66] There has been a serious scholarly debate concerning the appropriate interpretation of the phrase "faith of/in Jesus Christ" (πίστεως Ἰησοῦ Χριστοῦ). The substance of my interpretation in this book is not significantly affected by this debate. Thus the lay reader who chooses not to engage the subtleties of this debate will, in no way, be disadvantaged concerning my overall argument. The crux of this debate revolves around whether the phrase "faith of/in Jesus Christ" should be interpreted as a subjective or objective genitive. Greek is an "inflected language," which means that words adopt different "cases" and endings according to their grammatical usages in phrases and sentences. When one desires to reflect possession in Greek, one uses the genitive case (just as in English one might reflect possession by use of an apostrophe and an "s"). If the phrase "faith of/in Jesus Christ" is understood as a *subjective* genitive it would be translated as "faith *of* Jesus Christ," which would mean the faith(fulness) that Jesus Christ himself demonstrated by his submission to God's will, supremely manifested by death on the cross. Hence Jesus is the subject of the faith. On the other hand, if the phrase is understood as an *objective* genitive it would be translated as "faith *in* Jesus Christ," which would mean the believer's faithful acceptance of Jesus' sacrificial action. Hence Jesus is the object of the faith. For arguments for a subjective genitive interpretation see Richard B. Hays, *The Faith of Jesus Christ: An Investigation of the Narrative Substructure of*

Galatians 3:1–4:11 (Chico: Scholars, 1983), and George Howard, "Faith of Christ," *Anchor Bible Dictionary* (New York: Doubleday, 1992) 2:758–60. For arguments for an objective genitive interpretation see Arland Hultgren, "The *Pistis Christou* Formulation in Paul," *Novum Testamentum* XXII (1980) 248–63. As will be seen below, I construe the phrases in 2:16a and 2:16c as subjective genitives, where the faith of Jesus Christ is Pauline shorthand for the entire Christ event, that is, Paul's understanding of the story of God's work in Christ to provide for human and cosmic salvation. For further discussion of the importance of the "story of Christ" for Paul see Ben Witherington III, *Paul's Narrative Thought World: The Tapestry of Tragedy and Triumph* (Louisville: Westminster John Knox, 1994), especially 81–89 and 270.

[67] If one renders the phrase in question as an objective genitive, this creates a repetitive translation, so that 2:16 would read "[We] know that a person is not justified from the works of the law except through the faith *in* Jesus Christ. And we believed *in* Christ Jesus in order that we might be justified by the faith *in* Christ and not from the works of the law, because from the works of the law no flesh will be justified."

[68] Betz, *Galatians* 118.

[69] Dunn, *Jesus, Paul, and the Law* 224.

[70] Although there is no formal doctrine of the trinity in Paul's letters it is clear that he reflects on the functional relationships that exist among God, Christ, and the Spirit.

[71] For further discussion of African American Christian worship see Melva Wilson Costen, *African American Christian Worship* (Nashville: Abingdon, 1993), and Stewart, *Soul Survivors* 109–32.

[72] Trinity United Church of Christ's ethnically-centered approach to Christianity, which declares, "We are Unashamedly Black and Unapologetically Christian," has drawn the attention of another scholar, sociologist Andrew Billingsley. See Billingsley, *Mighty Like A River: The Black Church and Social Reform* (New York: Oxford University Press, 1999) 170–83.

[73] J. Frederick Holper, "Swimming in Unfamiliar Waters: What Can We Learn From Other Renewal Movements?" *Reformed Liturgy and Music* 31 (1997) 57.

[74] See Kelvin Shawn Sealey, ed., *Restoring Hope: Conversations on the Future of Black America* (Boston: Beacon, 1997) 40.

[75] The words "the gospel" do not actually occur in the Greek of Gal 3:2. They are, nevertheless, an appropriate rendering of the more wooden expression "the hearing of faith" (ἀκοῆς πίστεως). For further explanation see Daniel C. Arichea, Jr. and Eugene A. Nida, *A Translators' Handbook on Paul's Letter to the Galatians* (New York: United Bible Societies, 1975) 54–55.

[76] Ibid.

[77] Dunn, *Jesus, Paul, and The Law* 225.

[78] In the ancient world not only was there "social pressure" for Gentiles to be circumcised, there was also "social pressure" for Jews to be "un-circumcised." Uncircumcision could be accomplished by sewing a piece of flesh back onto the penis. The technical term for this surgical procedure was epispasm. First Maccabees 1:11-15, a Hellenistic Jewish text written in the first century B.C.E., discusses how certain extremely Hellenized Jews (i.e., Jews who were willing to utterly abandon their Jewish heritage in favor of being "Greek") submitted to epispasm, thus undoing their circumcision. For a classic exploration of the relationship between ancient Jewish and Greek cultures see Victor Tcherikover, *Hellenistic Civilization and the Jews* (Philadelphia: Jewish Publication Society of America, 1959). See also Peter Schäfer, *Judeophobia: Attitudes Towards the Jews in the Ancient World* (Cambridge, Mass.: Harvard University Press, 1997).

[79] For a discussion of some twentieth-century attempts by African Americans to "pass as white" see Alessandra Lorini, *Rituals of Race: American Public Culture and the Search for Racial Democracy* (Charlottesville: University Press of Virginia, 1999) 151–53.

[80] See Kathy Russell, Midge Wilson, and Ronald Hall, *The Color Complex: The Politics of Skin Color among African Americans* (New York: Harcourt Brace Jovanovich, 1992) 135–62.

[81] See Cheryl Townsend Gilkes, "The 'Loves' and 'Troubles' of African-American Women's Bodies," in Emilie M. Townes, ed., *A Troubling in My Soul: Womanist Perspectives on Evil and Suffering* (Maryknoll, N. Y.: Orbis, 1993) 232–49. Among other things, Gilkes explores the "color consciousness" that is still so prevalent in African American culture. When recounting the history of our racial struggles, older African Americans have mentioned to me the adage from the early and mid-twentieth century: "If you are light, you are all right. If you are brown, you can stick around, but if you are black step back." Unfortunately, this kind of color consciousness among African Americans is as prevalent in the twenty-first century as it was in the twentieth.

[82] This form of the verb "to know" (γινώσκετε) can be translated as an indicative or an imperative. I have translated it as an imperative.

[83] The words "the scripture says" are not in the Greek. I have inserted them to accentuate the fact that Paul is quoting from the Bible.

[84] Again I have inserted the explanatory phrase.

[85] Richard N. Longenecker, *Galatians* (Dallas: Word Books, 1990) 110.

[86] C. K. Barrett argued that Paul's opponents in Galatia introduced Abraham into the debate and quoted Gen 15:6 as support for their position. See Barrett, "The Allegory of Abraham, Sarah, and Hagar," in his *Essays on Paul* (London: S.P.C.K., 1982).

[87] I think that Paul considered the law still to be binding for Jews and even Jewish Christians. Thus I am basically in agreement with the so-called "new perspective" on Paul. The new perspective contends that when Paul offers negative comments about the law he is speaking generally about the effects of the law as it pertains to Gentile Christians, not Jews or Jewish Christians. Paul's protestations are not occasioned by the law per se, but rather by attempts to make the law normative for Gentile Christian existence. For a highly accessible account of the new perspective see John G. Gager, *Reinventing Paul* (New York: Oxford University Press, 2000), especially 43–75.

[88] Dunn, *Jesus, Paul, and the Law* 247.

[89] Betz, *Galatians* 144. Also, for a discussion of the importance of covenant theology in Paul's attitude toward the law see N. T. Wright, *The Climax of the Covenant: Christ and the Law in Pauline Theology* (Edinburgh: T & T Clark, 1991), especially Chapter 7.

[90] For a helpful discussion of 3:9-10 and of the alterations Paul makes in the biblical passages he quotes see Sam K. Williams, *Galatians* (Nashville: Abingdon, 1997) 88–90.

[91] Dunn, *Jesus, Paul, and the Law* 226.

[92] See Gal 3:21 and Rom 3:2; 7:7, 12.

[93] Again, for the Jewish Christian works of the law are not inherently problematic. But when they are divorced from faith, the works of the law could lead to a distorted perspective for the Jewish Christian. Moreover, the works of the law, when introduced to the Gentile Christian, would cause the Gentile Christian to focus more on the law than on the law's foundation, which is faith.

[94] Dunn, *Jesus, Paul, and the Law* 227.

[95] Ibid. 229–30.

[96] Randall Robinson offers a sobering analysis of how American mythology, monuments, and museums have conspired for centuries to mask the ineffable crimes against Africans and African Americans. Robinson describes a visit to the United States Capitol in Washington. Even though black slaves constructed this "monument to democracy and freedom," the Capitol pays no homage to its black constructors. To acknowledge the slaves' contributions would concomitantly compel America to confess how deeply the roots of American "freedom" are planted in the soil of slavery. Robinson writes: "This [the United States Capitol] was the house of Liberty, and it had been built by slaves. Their backs had ached under its massive stones. Their lungs had clogged with mortar dust. Their bodies had wilted under its load-bearing timbers. They had been paid only in the coin of pain. Slavery lay across American history like a monstrous cleaving sword, but the Capitol of the United States steadfastly refused to divulge its complicity, or even slavery's very occurrence. It

gave full lie to its own gold-spun half-truth." *The Debt: What America Owes to Blacks* (New York: Plume, 2000) 6.

[97] I distinguish here between the truth of the rhetoric in the Declaration of Independence and the actual beliefs held by the historical framers of that document. When the Declaration of Independence was written, blacks were not considered heirs of the promises of the inalienable rights of all humans. In 1776 blacks were not considered to be humans; they were thought to be chattel. Thomas Jefferson, the principal author of the text, was a slaveholder who believed that blacks were inferior to whites. Yet when the Declaration of Independence is loosed from its historical moorings its language can offer a penetrating critique of America. In a similar way, African Americans should see that Paul is loosing Abraham from his traditional moorings and offering Abraham as a critique against an improper understanding of the law.

[98] The jazz diva Billie Holiday protested the lynchings of African Americans in the early twentieth century with her song "Strange Fruit." She sang: "Southern trees bear strange fruit/ Blood on the leaves and blood at the root/ Black bodies swinging in the southern breeze/ Strange fruit hanging from the poplar trees."

[99] I am not an advocate of capital punishment. Yet one should take note of the disparity between the number of white Americans who have received capital punishment for the murder of an African American and the number of African Americans who have received capital punishment for the murder of a white American. Historically, in nearly every facet of American culture, including the criminal justice system, the dominant culture has sent the message that white people are more valuable and worth preserving than black people.

[100] The words translated as "the Gentiles" (τὰ ἔθνη) can also mean "the nations" or any "non-Jew." In this interpretation I have described certain white Americans analogously as "Judaizers" and African Americans as "Gentiles." Of course, historically in the American context even white Americans could be considered "Gentiles" in the sense that they are not indigenous Americans. The Native Americans were the first recipients of the richness and promise of this land. Moreover, historians have documented the interaction on the North American continent between Native Americans and Africans that occurred long before the "discovery" of Columbus in the late fifteenth century. Ironically, in contemporary race relations in America the ideal (or "original") American is often depicted as a white person. Yet centuries before European presence and domination became the norm in America, people of color inhabited and contributed to this land. See Ivan Van Sertima, ed., *African Presence in Early America* (New Brunswick: The Journal of African Civilizations, 1987).

[101] James H. Cone, *Black Theology and Black Power* (Enlarged ed. San Francisco: HarperSan Francisco, 1989) 69.

[102] Similar Pauline phrases that bear the same meaning include "in the Lord" (ἐν κυρίῳ) and "in Christ" (ἐν Χριστῷ).

[103] M. A. Seifrid, "In Christ," in Gerald F. Hawthorne, Ralph P. Martin, and Daniel G. Reid, eds., *Dictionary of Paul and His Letters* (Downers Grove, Ill.: Intervarsity Press, 1993) 436.

[104] See, for example, Wayne A. Meeks, "The Image of the Androgyne: Some Uses of a Symbol in Earliest Christianity," *History of Religions* 13 (1973) 165–208, and Elisabeth Schüssler Fiorenza, *In Memory of Her: A Feminist Theological Reconstruction of Christian Origins* (New York: Crossroad, 1983) 205–41.

[105] Longenecker, *Galatians* 156.

[106] In other contexts Paul addresses more directly the impact of social status (especially slavery) and gender relations. For his comments on slavery see, for example, 1 Cor 7:17-24 and Braxton, *The Tyranny of Resolution* 177–234. For Paul's comments on gender relationships see, for example, 1 Cor 7:1-16, 25-40 and 11:1-16. Also see Margaret Y. MacDonald, "Reading Real Women through the Undisputed Letters of Paul," 199–220, and Elizabeth A. Castelli, "Paul on Women and Gender," 221–35, in Ross Shepard Kraemer and Mary Rose D'Angelo, eds., *Women and Christian Origins* (New York: Oxford University Press, 1999).

[107] "Rhetorical situation" is a technical term describing the specific conditions or occurrences that compel speakers or writers to make particular responses. For further discussion see C. Clifton Black, "Rhetorical Criticism," in Joel B. Green, ed., *Hearing the New Testament: Strategies for Interpretation* (Grand Rapids: Eerdmans, 1995) 256–77.

[108] Although Paul believed that domination by virtue of ethnicity, social status, or gender should be absent from the Church, he struggled occasionally in his churches, especially with issues surrounding social status and gender relations. In 1 Corinthians 11 Paul criticizes the divisions that had arisen in the Church along economic lines. Also, given the significant presence of slaves in his churches, one can imagine some of the slaves saying to Paul: "The only way to truly ensure that our social status as slaves is not the basis of domination is to remove us from our status as slaves." Thus manumission may have been a pressing concern for some of Paul's converts. Moreover, the complexity of gender relations is also evident, for example, in 1 Corinthians 7, 11, and 14. For an intriguing interpretation of Paul's contentious statement about women in 1 Cor 14:34-35 see Craig S. Keener, *Paul, Women, and Wives: Marriage and Women's Ministry in the Letters of Paul* (Peabody, Mass.: Hendrickson, 1992) 70–100.

[109] See Beverly Roberts Gaventa, "Is Galatians Just a 'Guy Thing'?: A Theological Reflection," *Interpretation* 54 (July 2000) 267.

[110] For this idea I am indebted to Judith M. Gundry-Volf. I develop her notion, however, in a slightly different manner. See Gundry-Volf, "Christ and Gender: A Study of Difference and Equality in Gal 3:28," in Christof Landmesser, Hans-Joachim Eckstein, and Hermann Lichtenberger, eds., *Jesus Christus als die Mitte der Schrift* (Berlin: Walter de Gruyter, 1997) 439–77.

[111] William A. Jones, Jr., "The Struggle Against the System," in *The African American Church: Past, Present, and Future* (New York: Martin Luther King Fellows Press, 1991) 65.

[112] For a list of possible meanings of the term "the elements" (τὰ στοιχεῖα) see Longenecker, *Galatians* 165. Also see Walter Wink's treatment of "the elements" in *Unmasking the Powers: The Invisible Forces that Determine Human Existence* (Philadelphia: Fortress, 1986) 128–52.

[113] Gal 1:8-9.

[114] Gal 1:4.

[115] Betz, *Galatians* 214.

[116] Gal 3:7, 26-29.

[117] F. F. Bruce, *The Epistle to the Galatians* (Grand Rapids: Eerdmans, 1982) 205.

[118] Richard B. Hays, "The Letter to the Galatians," *The New Interpreter's Bible* (Nashville: Abingdon, 2000) 11:284.

[119] Betz, *Galatians* 206.

[120] For example, Exod 20:4-5, Ps 96:5, and Isa 2:6-8.

[121] See, for example, Gayraud S. Wilmore, *Black Religion and Black Radicalism* (3rd ed. Maryknoll, N.Y.: Orbis, 1998) 1–51.

[122] Kofi Asare Opoku, *West African Traditional Religion* (Accra, Ghana: FEP International Private Limited, 1978) 1.

[123] This phrase "not at all" is a translation of a grammatical construction designed to indicate the most emphatic form of negation (οὐ μὴ plus the subjunctive).

[124] Literally the Greek says "these things" (ταῦτα).

[125] Victor Paul Furnish, *Theology and Ethics in Paul* (Nashville: Abingdon, 1968) 13. For more recent discussions of the relationship between theology and ethics in Paul's letters see Eugene H. Lovering, Jr., and Jerry L. Sumney, eds., *Theology and Ethics in Paul and His Interpreters* (Nashville: Abingdon, 1996).

[126] John M. G. Barclay, *Obeying the Truth: A Study of Paul's Ethics in Galatians* (Edinburgh: T & T Clark, 1988) 58.

[127] Ibid. 60.

[128] Gal 4:17.

[129] For a treatment of the metaphor of slavery in early Christianity see Dale B. Martin, *Slavery as Salvation: The Metaphor of Slavery in Pauline Christianity* (New Haven: Yale University Press, 1990).

[130] Barclay, *Obeying the Truth* 109.

[131] Recall Paul's creative use of Abraham in 3:6-9.

[132] Longenecker, *Galatians* 243.

[133] Barclay, *Obeying the Truth* 142.

[134] For a classic discussion of the love command see Victor Paul Furnish, *The Love Command in the New Testament* (London: S.C.M. Press, 1973).

[135] See, for example, Gal 3:2-5 and 4:6.

[136] African American Christians have traditionally considered sin to be more than personal transgressions. Sin is a social reality that exists almost as an independent power. Although the concept of sin as a "power" does not receive full expression in Galatians, Paul speaks this way of sin in Romans. For example, see Rom 3:9 and 7:7-25.

[137] Jones, "The Struggle Against the System," 63.

[138] Longenecker, *Galatians* 259.

[139] The academy's suspicion about the validity of the slave narratives reveals the dominant ideology's view toward African Americans. For years it was nearly impossible for white academics to believe that the testimonies of black slaves (who in fact lived the experience of slavery) could be accurate and worthy of scholarly attention.

[140] Dwight N. Hopkins and George Cummings, eds., *Cut Loose Your Stammering Tongue: Black Theology in the Slave Narratives* (Maryknoll, N.Y.: Orbis, 1991) 49.

[141] For a similar interpretation of this passage in Mark see Ched Myers, *Binding the Strong Man: A Political Reading of Mark's Story of Jesus* (Maryknoll, N.Y.: Orbis, 1988) 261–62.

[142] These are lyrics from an African American spiritual. Deprived of many necessities of life, African American slaves envisioned another world where resources were distributed equitably to all God's children. This hope was not psychological escapism but apocalyptic hope that inspired them to protest against the injustices of *this* world.

[143] Cornel West, *Prophesy Deliverance! An Afro-American Revolutionary Christianity* (Philadelphia: Westminster, 1982) 15.

[144] Stephen D. Moore, *Literary Criticism and the Gospels: The Theoretical Challenge* (New Haven: Yale University Press, 1989) 124.

[145] From an African American spiritual.

Bibliography

A Greek-English Lexicon of the New Testament and Other Early Christian Literature (BAGD), edited by Frederick William Danker. Third Edition. Based on Walter Bauer's *Griechisch-deutsches Wörterbuch zu den Schriften des Neuen Testaments und der frühchristlichen Literatur*, Sixth Edition. Chicago and London: University of Chicago Press, 2000.

Achtemeier, Paul J. *Inspiration and Authority: Nature and Function of Christian Scripture.* Peabody, Mass.: Hendrickson, 1999.

Adam, A. K. M. *What Is Postmodern Biblical Criticism?* Minneapolis: Fortress, 1995.

Akbar, Na'im. *Visions for Black Men.* Tallahassee: Mind Productions and Associates, 1991.

Alexander, Loveday. "Chronology of Paul," in Gerald F. Hawthorne, Ralph P. Martin, and Daniel G. Reid, eds., *Dictionary of Paul and His Letters.* Downers Grove, Ill.: Intervarsity Press, 1993, 115–23.

Arichea, Daniel C., Jr., and Eugene A. Nida. *A Translators' Handbook on Paul's Letter to the Galatians.* New York: United Bible Societies, 1975.

Bailey, Randall C. "Academic Biblical Interpretation among African Americans in the United States," in Vincent L. Wimbush, ed., *African Americans and the Bible.* New York: Continuum, 2000, 696–711.

Bailey, Randall C., and Jacquelyn Grant, eds. *The Recovery of Black Presence: An Interdisciplinary Exploration.* Nashville: Abingdon, 1995.

Baldwin, James. *The Price of the Ticket.* New York: St. Martin's Press, 1985.

Banks, William M. *Black Intellectuals: Race and Responsibility in American Life.* New York: W. W. Norton & Company, 1996.

Barclay, John M. G. *Obeying the Truth: A Study of Paul's Ethics in Galatians.* Edinburgh: T & T Clark, 1988.

_____. *Jews in the Mediterranean Diaspora: From Alexander to Trajan (323 B.C.E.–117 C.E.)*. Edinburgh: T & T Clark, 1996.

Barr, James. *Escaping from Fundamentalism*. London: S.C.M. Press, 1984.

Barrett, C. K. "The Allegory of Abraham, Sarah, and Hagar," in idem, *Essays on Paul*. London: S.P.C.K., 1982.

_____. *Freedom & Obligation: A Study of the Epistle to the Galatians*. Philadelphia: Westminster, 1985.

Barthes, Roland. "From Work to Text," in Josué V. Harari, ed., *Textual Strategies: Perspectives in Post-Structural Criticism*. Ithaca: Cornell University Press, 1979, 73–81.

Betz, Hans Dieter. *Galatians: A Commentary on Paul's Letter to the Churches in Galatia*. Philadelphia: Fortress, 1979.

Billingsley, Andrew. *Mighty Like a River: The Black Church and Social Reform*. New York: Oxford University Press, 1999.

Black, C. Clifton. "Rhetorical Criticism," in Joel B. Green, ed., *Hearing the New Testament: Strategies for Interpretation*. Grand Rapids: Eerdmans, 1995, 256–77.

Boyarin, Daniel. *A Radical Jew: Paul and the Politics of Identity*. Berkeley: University of California Press, 1994.

Braxton, Brad Ronnell. *The Tyranny of Resolution: I Corinthians 7:17-24*. Atlanta: Society of Biblical Literature, 2000.

_____. "Guess Who's Coming to Dinner: The Black Jesus and Easter," *Chicago Tribune* (Friday, April 13, 2001).

Brown, Francis, S. R. Driver, and Charles A. Briggs. *A Hebrew and English Lexicon of the Old Testament*. Oxford: Clarendon Press, 1951.

Brown, Raymond E., and John P. Meier. *Antioch and Rome: New Testament Cradles of Catholic Christianity*. New York: Paulist, 1983.

Bruce, F. F. *The Epistle to the Galatians*. Grand Rapids: Eerdmans, 1982.

Brueggemann, Walter. *Texts Under Negotiation: The Bible and Postmodern Imagination*. Minneapolis: Fortress, 1993.

Burgess, John P. *Why Scripture Matters: Reading the Bible in a Time of Church Conflict*. Louisville: Westminster John Knox, 1998.

Campbell, William S. "Judaizers," in Gerald F. Hawthorne, Ralph P. Martin, and Daniel G. Reid, eds., *Dictionary of Paul and His Letters*. Downers Grove, Ill.: Intervarsity Press, 1993, 512–16.

Castelli, Elizabeth A. "Paul on Women and Gender," in Ross Shepard Kraemer and Mary Rose D'Angelo, eds., *Women and Christian Origins*. New York: Oxford University Press, 1999, 221–35.

Charlesworth, James H., ed. *The Old Testament Pseudepigrapha*. 2 vols. New York: Doubleday, 1983.

Collins, Patricia Hill. *Black Feminist Thought: Knowledge, Consciousness, and the Politics of Empowerment*. New York: Routledge, 1990.

Combrink, H. J. Bernard. "The Rhetoric of Sacred Scripture," in Stanley E. Porter and Thomas H. Olbricht, eds., *Rhetoric, Scripture and Theology*. Sheffield: Sheffield Academic Press, 1996, 102–23.

Cone, James H. *The Spirituals and the Blues*. Maryknoll, N.Y.: Orbis, 1972.

_____. *Black Theology and Black Power*. Enlarged ed. San Francisco: HarperSan Francisco, 1989.

_____. "Black Theology as Liberation," in Gayraud S. Wilmore, ed., *African American Religious Studies: An Interdisciplinary Anthology*. Durham, N.C.: Duke University Press, 1989.

Costen, Melva Wilson. *African American Christian Worship*. Nashville: Abingdon, 1993.

Croatto, J. Severino. *Biblical Hermeneutics: Toward a Theory of Reading as the Production of Meaning*. Maryknoll, N.Y.: Orbis, 1987.

Crowder, Michael. *West Africa: An Introduction to its History*. London: Longman, 1977.

Cummings, George C. L. "New Voices in Black Theology: The African-American Story as a Source of Emancipatory Rhetoric," in James H. Cone and Gayraud S. Wilmore, eds., *Black Theology: A Documentary History*. Maryknoll, N.Y.: Orbis, 1993, 2:71–75.

De Ste. Croix, Geoffrey Ernest Maurice. *The Class Struggle in the Ancient Greek World: From the Archaic Age to the Arab Conquest*. Ithaca: Cornell University Press, 1981.

DeVries, LaMoine F. *Cities of the Biblical World*. Peabody, Mass.: Hendrickson, 1998.

Dorbin, Sidney I. "Race and the Public Intellectual: A Conversation with Michael Eric Dyson," in Gary A. Olson and Lynn Worsham, eds., *Race, Rhetoric, and the Postcolonial*. Albany: State University of New York Press, 1999, 81–126.

Douglas, Kelly Brown. "Womanist Theology: What Is Its Relationship to Black Theology?" in James H. Cone and Gayraud S. Wilmore, eds., *Black Theology: A Documentary History*. Maryknoll, N.Y.: Orbis, 1993, 2:290–99.

_____. *Sexuality and the Black Church: A Womanist Perspective*. Maryknoll, N.Y.: Orbis, 1999.

Douglass, Frederick. "The Significance of Emancipation in the West Indies," August 3, 1857, in John W. Blassingame, ed., *The Frederick Douglass Papers*. Series One, Volume 3. New Haven: Yale University Press, 1985.

Du Bois, W. E. B. *The Souls of Black Folk*. Chicago: A. C. McClurg and Co., 1903; reprint New York: Dover Publications, 1994.

Dunn, James D. G. *Jesus, Paul, and the Law: Studies in Mark and Galatians*. London: S.P.C.K., 1990.

———. "The Theology of Galatians: The Issue of Covenantal Nomism," in Jouette M. Bassler, ed., *Pauline Theology: Thessalonians, Philippians, Galatians, Philemon*. Minneapolis: Fortress Press, 1991, 125–46.

Dyson, Michael Eric. "Gangsta Rap and American Culture," in idem, *Between God and Gangsta Rap: Bearing Witness to Black Culture*. New York: Oxford University Press, 1996.

Eagleton, Terry. *Literary Theory: An Introduction*. Minneapolis: University of Minnesota Press, 1983.

———. *Ideology*. London: Verso, 1991.

Feagin, Joe R. "Fighting White Racism: The Future of Equal Rights in the United States," in Samuel L. Myers, Jr., ed., *Civil Rights and Race Relations in the Post Reagan-Bush Era*. Westport, Conn.: Praeger, 1997, 29–45.

Felder, Cain Hope, ed. *Stony the Road We Trod: African American Biblical Interpretation*. Minneapolis: Fortress, 1991.

Fish, Stanley. *Is There a Text in This Class? The Authority of Interpretive Communities*. Cambridge, Mass.: Harvard University Press, 1980.

———. *Doing What Comes Naturally: Change, Rhetoric, and the Practice of Theory in Literary and Legal Studies*. Durham, N.C.: Duke University Press, 1989.

Foner, Philip, ed. *W. E. B. Du Bois Speaks, 1890–1919*. 2 vols. New York: Pathfinder Press, 1970.

Fowl, Stephen. "The Ethics of Interpretation or What's Left Over After the Elimination of Meaning," *Society of Biblical Literature Seminar Papers*. Atlanta: Scholars Press, 1988, 69–81.

Franklin, Robert Michael. *Liberating Visions: Human Fulfillment and Social Justice in African-American Thought*. Minneapolis: Fortress, 1990.

Furnish, Victor Paul. *Theology and Ethics in Paul*. Nashville: Abingdon, 1968.

———. *The Love Command in the New Testament*. London: S.C.M. Press, 1973.

Gadamer, Hans-Georg. *Truth and Method.* London: Sheed & Ward, 1975.

Gager, John G. *The Origins of Anti-Semitism: Attitudes Toward Judaism in Pagan and Christian Antiquity.* New York: Oxford University Press, 1983.

_____. *Reinventing Paul.* New York: Oxford University Press, 2000.

Gamble, Harry Y. *The New Testament Canon: Its Making and Meaning.* Philadelphia: Fortress, 1985.

_____. *Books and Readers in the Early Church: A History of Early Christian Texts.* New Haven: Yale University Press, 1995.

Gates, Henry Louis, Jr. *The Signifying Monkey: A Theory of Afro-American Literary Criticism.* New York: Oxford University Press, 1988.

Gaventa, Beverly Roberts. "Is Galatians Just a 'Guy Thing'?: A Theological Reflection," *Interpretation* 54 (July 2000) 267–78.

Genovese, Eugene D. *Roll Jordan Roll: The World the Slaves Made.* New York: Vintage Books, 1974.

Gilkes, Cheryl Townsend. "The 'Loves' and 'Troubles' of African-American Women's Bodies," in Emilie M. Townes, ed., *A Troubling in My Soul: Womanist Perspectives on Evil and Suffering.* Maryknoll, N.Y.: Orbis, 1993, 232–49.

Grabbe, Lester L. *Leviticus.* Sheffield: Sheffield Academic Press, 1993.

Gundry-Volf, Judith M. "Christ and Gender: A Study of Difference and Equality in Gal 3:28," in Christof Landmesser, Hans-Joachim Eckstein, and Hermann Lichtenberger, eds., *Jesus Christus als die Mitte der Schrift.* Berlin: Walter de Gruyter, 1997, 439–77.

Harding, Vincent. "Religion and Resistance among Antebellum Slaves, 1800–1860," in Timothy E. Fulop and Albert J. Raboteau, eds., *African-American Religion: Interpretive Essays in History and Culture.* New York: Routledge, 1997, 107–30.

Hauerwas, Stanley. *Unleashing the Scripture: Freeing the Bible from Captivity to America.* Nashville: Abingdon, 1993.

Hays, Richard B. *The Faith of Jesus Christ: An Investigation of the Narrative Substructure of Galatians 3:1–4:11.* Chico: Scholars, 1983.

_____. "Christology and Ethics in Galatians: The Law of Christ," *Catholic Biblical Quarterly* 49 (1987) 268–90.

_____. *Echoes of Scripture in the Letters of Paul.* New Haven: Yale University Press, 1989.

_____. "The Letter to the Galatians," *The New Interpreter's Bible.* Nashville: Abingdon, 2000, 11:181–348.

Herzog, Frederick. *Liberation Theology: Liberation in the Light of the Fourth Gospel.* New York: Seabury, 1972.

Heschel, Abraham J. *The Prophets.* New York: HarperCollins, 1962.

Holper, J. Frederick. "Swimming in Unfamiliar Waters: What Can We Learn from Other Renewal Movements?" *Reformed Liturgy and Music* 31 (1997) 52–57.

Holtz, Barry W. "Midrash," in idem, ed., *Back to the Sources: Reading the Classic Jewish Texts.* New York: Summit Books, 1984.

hooks, bell. *Yearning: race, gender, and cultural politics.* Boston: South End Press, 1990.

Hopkins, Dwight N., and George Cummings, eds. *Cut Loose Your Stammering Tongue: Black Theology in the Slave Narratives.* Maryknoll, N.Y.: Orbis, 1991.

Howard, George. *Paul: Crisis in Galatia: A Study in Early Christian Theology.* Cambridge: Cambridge University Press, 1979.

_____. "Faith of Christ," in David Noel Freedman, ed., *Anchor Bible Dictionary.* New York: Doubleday, 1992, 2:758–60.

Hultgren, Arland J. "The *Pistis Christou* Formulation in Paul," *Novum Testamentum* 22 (1980) 248–63.

Jewett, Robert. *A Chronology of Paul's Life.* Philadelphia: Fortress, 1979.

Johnson, Luke T. *Religious Experience in Earliest Christianity.* Minneapolis: Fortress, 1998.

_____. *The Writings of the New Testament: An Interpretation.* Revised edition. Minneapolis: Fortress, 1999.

Jones, William A., Jr. "The Struggle Against the System," in Harold A. Carter, Wyatt Tee Walker, and William A. Jones, Jr., *The African American Church: Past, Present and Future.* New York: Martin Luther King Fellows Press, 1991, 60–80.

Jones, William R. "Theodicy: The Controlling Category for Black Theology," *The Journal of Religious Thought* 30 (1973) 28–38.

Keener, Craig S. *Paul, Women, and Wives: Marriage and Women's Ministry in the Letters of Paul.* Peabody, Mass.: Hendrickson, 1992.

Kelsey, David H. *The Uses of Scripture in Recent Theology.* Philadelphia: Fortress, 1975.

Kermode, Frank. *The Genesis of Secrecy: On the Interpretation of Narrative.* Cambridge, Mass.: Harvard University Press, 1979.

King, Martin Luther Jr. *Strength to Love.* Philadelphia: Fortress, 1963.

Kirk-Duggan, Cheryl A. *Exorcizing Evil: A Womanist Perspective on the Spirituals.* Maryknoll, N.Y.: Orbis, 1997.

Kraftchick, Steven J. "Facing Janus: Reviewing the Biblical Theology Movement," in Steven J. Kraftchick, Charles D. Myers, Jr., and Ben

C. Ollenburger, eds., *Biblical Theology: Problems and Perspectives.* Nashville: Abindgon, 1995, 54–77.

Kugel, James L., and Rowan A. Greer. *Early Biblical Interpretation.* Philadelphia: Westminster, 1986.

Landrine, Hope, and Elizabeth A. Klonoff. *African American Acculturation: Deconstructing Race and Reviving Culture.* Thousand Oaks, Calif.: Sage Publications, 1996.

Lincoln, C. Eric. *Race, Religion, and the Continuing American Dilemma.* New York: Hill and Wang, 1984.

_____. *The Black Muslims in America.* 3rd ed. Grand Rapids: Eerdmans, 1994.

Long, Thomas G. *The Witness of Preaching.* Louisville: Westminster John Knox, 1989.

Long, Tim. "A Real Reader Reading Revelation," *Semeia* 73 (1996) 79–107.

Longenecker, Richard N. *Galatians.* Dallas: Word Books, 1990.

Lorini, Alessandra. *Rituals of Race: American Public Culture and the Search for Racial Democracy.* Charlottesville: University Press of Virginia, 1999.

Lovering, Eugene H. Jr., and Jerry L. Sumney, eds. *Theology and Ethics in Paul and His Interpreters.* Nashville: Abingdon, 1996.

MacDonald, Margaret Y. "Reading Real Women through the Undisputed Letters of Paul," in Ross Shepard Kraemer and Mary Rose D'Angelo, eds., *Women and Christian Origins.* New York: Oxford University Press, 1999, 199–220.

Martin, Clarice J. "Biblical Theodicy and Black Women's Spiritual Autobiography," in Emilie M. Townes, ed., *A Troubling in My Soul: Womanist Perspectives on Evil and Suffering.* Maryknoll, N.Y.: Orbis, 1993, 13–36.

Martin, Dale B. *Slavery as Salvation: The Metaphor of Slavery in Pauline Christianity.* New Haven: Yale University Press, 1990.

Martyn, J. Louis. *Galatians.* AB 33a. New York: Doubleday, 1997.

Matera, Frank J. *Galatians.* Collegeville: The Liturgical Press, 1992.

McDonald, Lee Martin. *The Formation of the Christian Biblical Canon.* Nashville: Abingdon, 1988.

McKnight, Edgar V. "Reader-Response Criticism," in Steven L. McKenzie and Stephen R. Haynes, eds., *To Each Its Own Meaning: Biblical Criticisms and Their Application.* Louisville: Westminster John Knox, 1999, 230–52.

McMickle, Marvin A. *Preaching to the Black Middle Class: Words of Challenge, Words of Hope.* Valley Forge, Pa.: Judson Press, 2000.

Meeks, Wayne A. "The Image of the Androgyne: Some Uses of a Symbol in Earliest Christianity," *History of Religions* 13 (1973) 165–208.

Moore, Stephen D. *Literary Criticism and the Gospels: The Theoretical Challenge.* New Haven: Yale University Press, 1989.

Morgan, Robert (with John Barton). *Biblical Interpretation.* Oxford: Oxford University Press, 1988.

Mosala, Itumeleng J. *Biblical Hermeneutics and Black Theology in South Africa.* Grand Rapids: Eerdmans, 1989.

Myers, Ched. *Binding the Strong Man: A Political Reading of Mark's Story of Jesus.* Maryknoll, N.Y.: Orbis, 1988.

Myers, William H. "The Hermeneutical Dilemma of the African American Biblical Student," in Cain Hope Felder, ed., *Stony the Road We Trod: African American Biblical Interpretation.* Minneapolis: Fortress, 1991, 40–56.

Ogden, Schubert M. *Doing Theology Today.* Valley Forge, Pa.: Trinity Press International, 1996.

Oglesby, E. Hammond. *O Lord, Move This Mountain: Racism and Christian Ethics.* St. Louis: Chalice Press, 1998.

Olson, Gary A. "Fish Tales: A Conversation with 'The Contemporary Sophist,'" in idem, ed., *Philosophy, Rhetoric, Literary Criticism: (Inter)views.* Carbondale: Southern Illinois University Press, 1994.

Omi, Michael, and Howard Winant. "Racial Formations," in Paul S. Rotherberg, ed., *Race, Class, and Gender in the United States: An Integrated Study.* New York: St. Martin's Press, 1998, 13–22.

Opoku, Kofi Asare. *West African Traditional Religion.* Accra, Ghana: FEP International Private Limited, 1978.

Paris, Peter J. *The Social Teaching of the Black Churches.* Philadelphia: Fortress, 1985.

———. *The Spirituality of African Peoples: The Search for a Common Moral Discourse.* Minneapolis: Fortress, 1995.

Patte, Daniel. "Acknowledging the Contextual Character of Male, European-American Critical Exegeses: An Androcritical Perspective," in Fernando F. Sevogia and Mary Ann Tolbert, eds., *Reading from This Place: Social Location and Biblical Interpretation in the United States.* Minneapolis: Fortress, 1995, 35–55.

Pinn, Anthony B. *Varieties of African American Religious Experience.* Minneapolis: Fortress, 1998.

Raboteau, Albert J. *Slave Religion: The "Invisible Institution" in the Antebellum South.* New York: Oxford University Press, 1978.

Ramsey, Boniface. *Beginning to Read the Fathers.* New York: Paulist, 1985.

Reid, Stephen Breck. *Experience and Tradition: A Primer in Black Biblical Hermeneutics.* Nashville: Abingdon, 1990.

Rensberger, David. *Johannine Faith and Liberating Community.* Philadelphia: Westminster, 1988.

Riggs, Marcia Y., ed. *Can I Get a Witness? Prophetic Religious Voices of African American Women.* Maryknoll, N.Y.: Orbis, 1997.

Robbins, Vernon K. *Exploring the Texture of Texts: A Guide to Socio-Rhetorical Interpretation.* Valley Forge, Pa.: Trinity Press International, 1996.

Roberts, J. Deotis. *Liberation and Reconciliation: A Black Theology.* Philadelphia: Westminster, 1971.

Robinson, Randall. *The Debt: What America Owes to Blacks.* New York: Plume, 2000.

Roetzel, Calvin J. *Paul: The Man and the Myth.* Columbia, S.C.: University of South Carolina Press, 1998.

Rowland, Christopher, ed. *The Cambridge Companion to Liberation Theology.* Cambridge: Cambridge University Press, 1999.

Russell, Kathy, Midge Wilson, and Ronald Hall. *The Color Complex: The Politics of Skin Color among African Americans.* New York: Harcourt Brace Jovanovich, 1992.

Sanders, E. P. *Paul and Palestinian Judaism: A Comparison of Patterns of Religion.* London: S.C.M. Press, 1977.

Saye, Scott C. "The Wild and Crooked Tree: Barth, Fish, and Interpretive Communities," *Modern Theology* 12 (1996) 435–58.

Schäfer, Peter. *Judeophobia: Attitudes towards the Jews in the Ancient World.* Cambridge, Mass.: Harvard University Press, 1997.

Schiffman, Lawrence H. *Texts and Traditions: A Source Reader for the Study of Second Temple and Rabbinic Judaism.* Hoboken, N.J.: Ktav Publishing House, 1998.

Schneemelcher, Wilhelm, ed. *The New Testament Apocrypha.* 2 vols. Philadelphia: Westminster, 1964.

Schneiders, Sandra M. *The Revelatory Text: Interpreting the New Testament as Sacred Scripture.* San Francisco: HarperSan Francisco, 1991. 2nd ed. Collegeville: The Liturgical Press, 1999.

Schüssler Fiorenza, Elisabeth. *In Memory of Her: Feminist Theological Reconstruction of Christian Origins.* New York: Crossroad, 1983.

Scroggs, Robin. "The Bible as Foundational Document," *Interpretation* 49 (January 1995) 17–30.

Sealey, Kelvin Shawn, ed. *Restoring Hope: Conversations on the Future of Black America.* Boston: Beacon, 1997.

Seifrid, M. A. "In Christ," in Gerald F. Hawthorne, Ralph P. Martin, and Daniel G. Reid, eds., *Dictionary of Paul and His Letters.* Downers Grove, Ill.: Intervarsity Press, 1993, 433–36.

Smith, Theophus H. *Conjuring Culture: Biblical Formations of Black America.* New York: Oxford University Press, 1994.

Sobel, Mechal. *Trabelin' On: The Slave Journey to an Afro-Baptist Faith.* Princeton, N.J.: Princeton University Press, 1979.

Stendahl, Krister. *Paul among Jews and Gentiles.* Philadelphia: Fortress, 1977.

Stewart, Carlyle Fielding III. *Soul Survivors: An African American Spirituality.* Louisville: Westminster John Knox, 1997.

Tcherikover, Victor. *Hellenistic Civilization and the Jews.* Translated by S. Applebaum. Philadelphia: The Jewish Publication Society of America, 1959.

Thernstrom, Stephan, and Abigail Thernstrom. *America in Black and White: One Nation, Indivisible.* New York: Simon & Schuster, 1997.

Thiselton, Anthony C. *New Horizons in Hermeneutics: The Theory and Practice of Transforming Biblical Reading.* Grand Rapids: Zondervan, 1992.

Townes, Emilie M., ed. *Embracing the Spirit: Womanist Perspectives on Hope, Salvation, and Transformation.* Maryknoll, N.Y.: Orbis, 1997.

Unander, Dave. *Shattering the Myth of Race: Genetic Realities and Biblical Truths.* Valley Forge, Pa.: Judson Press, 2000.

Van Sertima, Ivan, ed. *African Presence in Early America.* New Brunswick, N.J.: The Journal of African Civilizations, 1987.

Vanhoozer, Kevin J. *Is There a Meaning in This Text?* Grand Rapids: Zondervan, 1998.

Walker, Alice. *In Search of Our Mother's Gardens.* New York: Harcourt, Brace, Jovanovich, 1983.

West, Cornel. *Prophesy Deliverance! An Afro-American Revolutionary Christianity.* Philadelphia: Westminster, 1982.

_____. *Race Matters.* Boston: Beacon, 1993.

Williams, Delores S. *Sisters in the Wilderness: The Challenge of Womanist God-Talk.* Maryknoll, N.Y.: Orbis, 1993.

Williams, Sam K. *Galatians.* Nashville: Abingdon, 1997.

Wilmore, Gayraud S. *Black Religion and Black Radicalism.* 3rd ed. Maryknoll, N.Y.: Orbis, 1998.

Wimbush, Vincent L. "Biblical Historical Study as Liberation: Toward an Afro-Christian Hermeneutic," in Gayraud S. Wilmore, ed., *African American Religious Studies: An Interdisciplinary Anthology.* Durham, N.C.: Duke University Press, 1989, 140–54.

_____. "The Bible and African Americans: An Outline of an Interpretive History," in Cain Hope Felder, ed., *Stony the Road We Trod: African American Biblical Interpretation.* Minneapolis: Fortress, 1991, 81–97.

_____, ed. *African Americans and the Bible: Sacred Texts and Social Textures.* New York: Continuum, 2000.

Wink, Walter. *The Bible in Human Transformation: Toward a New Paradigm for Biblical Study.* Philadelphia: Fortress, 1973.

_____. *Unmasking the Powers: The Invisible Forces that Determine Human Existence.* Philadelphia: Fortress, 1986.

Witherington, Ben III. *Paul's Narrative Thought World: The Tapestry of Tragedy and Triumph.* Louisville: Westminster John Knox, 1994.

Woodson, Carter G. *The Mis-Education of the Negro.* Washington, D.C.: Associated Publishers, 1933; reprint Trenton, N.J.: African World Press, 2000.

Wright, Jeremiah A. *Africans Who Shaped Our Faith.* Chicago: Urban Ministries, 1995.

Wright, N. T. *The Climax of the Covenant: Christ and the Law in Pauline Theology.* Edinburgh: T & T Clark, 1991.

Index